CW00339938

Memories
of
Ipswich

Part of the
Memories
series

*The Publishers would like to thank the following companies for supporting
the production of this book*

Main Sponsor
Mason's Paper

Alstons

J Breheny (Contractors) Limited

RG Carter Group

HO Cox

Ensors

Farthing Singleton & Hastings

Guardian Insurance

Ipswich Building Society

Jackaman, Smith & Mulley

Jackson Group plc

P&O Ferrymasters

Textron Turf Care and Speciality Products

Titchmarsh & Goodwin

First published in Great Britain by True North Books Limited
Units 3 - 5 Heathfield Industrial Park
Elland West Yorkshire
HX5 9AE
Tel. 01422 377977
© Copyright: True North Books Limited 1999

ISBN 1 900463 09 1

*Text, design and origination by True North Books Limited
Printed and bound by The Amadeus Press Limited*

Memories are made of this

Memories. We all have them; some good, some bad, but our memories of the town we grew up in are usually tucked away in a very special place in our minds. The best are usually connected with our childhood and youth, when we longed to be grown up and paid no attention to adults who told us to enjoy being young, as these were the best years of our lives. We look back now and realise that they were right.

So many memories - perhaps of the war and rationing, perhaps of parades, celebrations and Royal visits. And so many changes; one-way traffic systems and pedestrianisation. New trends in shopping led that to the very first self-serve stores being opened.

Through the bad times and the good, however, Ipswich not only survived but prospered. We have only to look at the town as it is today, with its exciting developments in sport and leisure, shopping and the arts, to see what progress has been realised and what achievements have been made over the last 50 years. Ipswich has a history to be proud of - but more importantly, a great future to look forward to, into the new millennium and beyond.

Contents

The streets of change

Above: We could easily use this unfamiliar view to play the game 'Where is it?'; how many of our younger readers have recognised this 1940s scene as Fore Hamlet? Little remains of this view today; the trolley bus on the left is passing the only surviving building. A tight bunch of cyclists (inappropriately dressed by today's style of cycling wear!) has just passed the little tobacconists at the end of Cavendish Street, and are heading for Bishops Hill. The leading cyclist, complete with cycle clips, sports a wicker basket fixed to the front of his bike. Not quite the thing today, though perfectly acceptable in the 1940s. Will the lorry be stuck behind the bikes all the way up the hill, we wonder - or will it be travelling even slower than they are? The tobacconist advertises Wills Woodbines, which later acquired the label 'The great little cigarette', while the gable end of the opposite house carries a typical 1940s poster

plugging the benefits of saving. During World War II the public were bombarded with slogans that rained down on them as thickly as German bombs: 'Dig for victory!'; 'Britain can take it!'; 'Careless talk costs lives'; 'Make do and mend'. The posters that were designed to boost morale and keep people security conscious appeared on every available advertisement hoarding.

Top: Like Big Brother, a rather unnerving pair of eyes gazes down from opticians Burcham & Croydon, keeping tabs on the passers-by in the Buttermarket. Eyes were obviously in the fashion in advertising one's services back in 1949, when this photograph was taken; a single eye is mounted outside another shop further along the street. A nearby sign reveals that it was perhaps this establishment which was devoted to facial treatment, ladies' hairdressing and electrolysis. Further along The Buttermarket - and just creeping into the photograph - is the Ancient House, a Grade I Listed Building. One of Ipswich's many historical buildings, the Ancient House has a very picturesque past. Earlier structures still survive within the building which date back as far as the 1400s. King Charles II, so it is said, took refuge here in 1651 after being defeated at the Battle of Worcester. It is the lovely old vehicles in the foreground, however, that immediately capture one's attention; think how much the sleek Standard convertible or the shiny Rover parked next to it would be worth now! The Buttermarket is still recognisable today, though the splendid Buttermarket Shopping Centre has been added to the town since that time. The bank on the corner was later demolished and the site acquired by the Yorkshire Bank.

Bottom: How many readers remember the Milk Bar in St Matthews Street? Across the length and breadth of the country, Milk Bars had become a common sight in virtually every high street. An ideal place to pop in for a glass of milk, a quick cup of tea or coffee, and a snack, these pleasant and cosy establishments remained popular until the late 50s. When this photograph was taken, around 1960, they had already begun to give way to the 'coffee bar', whose very name sounded so much more sophisticated than the label 'milk bar', which began to be regarded as countrified and 'backwoodsy'.

A rather nice Standard 12 is about to pass the premises of Howes car dealers, whose car park lay to the rear of the building. The Queens Head on the right had a history that stretched back to the 1680s, when it was a private house, though by the early 18th century it had become the Queen's Head, well known for the cock-fighting that went on in its back room. These properties were later demolished in the early 1960s to make way for Civic Drive. Outside the pub, two little boys - whose clothing reflected the fashion of the day - have spotted the camera. Both boys are wearing short trousers (which were to die a death not many years on); and is that a leather helmet worn by the boy on the left? Today's youngsters may find it hard to believe that leather helmets were once popular headgear!

Right: 'Look - no hands!' No hands, no feet - and no safety net either! Australian acrobat Eddie Ash was so confident in his skills that he made standing on his head on the narrow parapet atop the Hippodrome Theatre look as effortless and danger-free as relaxing in an easy chair. If his performance was intended to be a publicity stunt, however, it was unfortunately destined to failure, as the lack of interest from passers-by have

turned it into a non-event. Perhaps a few posters announcing his intention would have done the trick? The old theatre in St Peters Street had been a favourite place for an evening out since it was opened as a music hall back in 1905. The Hippodrome will always be a very special place to many of our readers, a mixture of plays, pantomimes and musicals weaving themselves into their memories across the years. Remember the pantomimes we saw there as children? Interactive or what! Boos and hisses. Cinderella and Buttons; the fairy godmother; the ugly sisters and, of course, the prince, complete with shapely legs and high heels. The times we shouted 'He's behind you!' and responded to the inevitable 'Oh no he isn't' with 'Oh yes he is!' Great stuff. The Hippodrome closed as a theatre in 1957 and became the Savoy Ballroom, eventually going 'eyes down' to bingo. It gradually relinquished its hold on life and was demolished in 1985.

Should this photograph perhaps be labelled 'Directions for Dummies'? Motorists emerging from Lloyds Avenue could hardly mistake the way they should go, which was well laid out for them by a line of thickly-sprinkled arrows. Footmans drapery and furnishings store occupied most of the building adjacent to Lloyds Avenue at the time of the photograph - the late 1950s. It was eventually acquired by Debenhams. Clinton Cards today occupies the fine building that was once the premises of

In the 50s Footmans drapery store occupied most of the building adjacent to Lloyds Avenue

J H Grimwade & Son, the well known outfitters. Here the shop's sun blinds proudly announce that they are agents for the prestigious Jaeger name. In earlier days the proprietor John Grimwade produced an elaborate trade card that proudly pictured this rather stately building on the corner of Westgate Street and Cornhill, describing himself as a 'Merchant Tailor, Woollen Draper, Hatter & Hosier'. Grimwade later acquired the adjoining property and extended what had become a flourishing business.

A glance at the 1930s

WHAT'S ON?

In this heyday of the cinema, horrified audiences were left gasping at the sight of Fay Wray in the clutches of the giant ape in the film 'King Kong', released in 1933. Very different but just as gripping was the gutsy 1939 American Civil War romance 'Gone with the Wind'. Gable's parting words, 'Frankly, my dear, I don't give a damn' went down in history.

GETTING AROUND

At the beginning of the decade many believed that the airship was the transport of the future. The R101 airship, however, loaded with thousands of cubic metres of hydrogen, crashed in France on its maiden flight in 1930. Forty-eight passengers and crew lost their lives. In 1937 the Hindenburg burst into flames - the entire disaster caught on camera and described by a distraught reporter. The days of the airship were numbered.

SPORTING CHANCE

The black American Jesse Owens won a brilliant four world records in the 1936 Olympic Games in Berlin, thumbing the nose to Adolph Hitler's dreams of Aryan superiority. In a petty display Hitler walked out of the stadium and 'took his bat home'; later he refused to have his photograph taken with the victorious Owens.

Isn't it amazing how familiarity can breed, if not contempt, at least inattention? Passers-by on the Cornhill are obviously so used to seeing the Town Hall that they rarely if ever stop to admire the beautiful Italian-style building, which is now more than 100 years old. The building was opened in 1868 at a cost of £16,000 - which seems a snip at today's prices but was a huge amount of money back then! Built from a variety of materials - Portland stone,

red sandstone and Bath stone, the crowning glory of the building is its elegant, 120ft clock tower and the four feminine figures of Agriculture, Learning, Justice and Commerce that rise above the portico. Nearby, the Golden Lion reminds us of an even earlier time, as the old inn found its way into records dating from 1579. Back then it was a regular stop for the coaches 'Volunteer' and 'Telegraph', who changed their horses there on the Yarmouth route.

Over the years the public house has been restored, renovated and modernised to keep pace with changing times.

On the far right of the photograph we can spot one of the town's early single-deck trolley buses; note the advertising boards mounted on top. When these trolley buses were scrapped Number 44 of the fleet went on to become an exhibit in the Museum of British Transport in Clapham.

The services of this white coated traffic policeman appear to be largely redundant, as there seem to be far more pedestrians than traffic about in this photograph that dates from 1951. A line of passengers queues to board the bus on the Cornhill; a familiar enough scene at the time, when both motor buses and trolley buses waited at this spot. Only the feet of passers-by pass through Lloyds Avenue on to the Cornhill today. This has long been the heart of Ipswich's shopping area; Burtons gents outfitters was off the far right of the picture; their stores were all built to the same typical design across the length and breadth of the country. Timpson was only one of a large number of shoe shops in the town; is it imagination, or are there far fewer specialist shoe shops around today than there used to be? Passing in front of the arched avenue, an informative sign on the left directs passers by to the Natural History Museum and the Public Baths. The lively Museum in High Street remains popular, with residents as well as visitors, and events and special exhibitions are still staged regularly.

Palace. One hundred years on, several buildings were constructed in London to mark the Festival's centenary, including the prestigious Royal Festival Hall and an exciting structure called the Skylon, which rose 300 feet above the exhibition grounds; illuminated at night, the Skylon was visible for miles around. A vast Dome of Discovery, intended to be a visible sign of national achievement, was built.

Top: A trip down memory lane.... This was Westgate Street in the 1950s, when traffic was still able to travel in the direction of Barrack Corner, and parking was still allowed, though only between certain hours. A taxi has stopped outside the two star Crown and Anchor Hotel, either dropping off hotel clients or picking them up to carry them away to the railway station. The Crown and Anchor - a Trust House Hotel - was a well known stopping off place for visitors to Ipswich, and was both AA and RAC registered. The frontage appears to have been modest for a hotel that had a total of 47 bedrooms, but their premises actually stretched out above the nearby ground floor shops. What would a bed for the night have set you back in the 1950s? A decade on, bed and breakfast at the Crown and Anchor was listed at a modest £2, with lunches from 12/6d (around 62p). Lovers of trivia might enjoy remembering that although coach parties were not encouraged to drop off there, at least you could take your dog with you.... The hotel has now been converted to shops. The scene has changed little today except for the obvious fact that Westgate Street is now a pedestrian precinct. The names above the shops, too, have changed, and the Crown and Anchor is now a branch of W H Smith.

Above: This nostalgic shot of the Cornhill was taken in 1951, and reveals a scene that was very different from the same view today. Tavern Street was congested with traffic, with private cars, commercial vehicles and a trolley bus all making their way past the central Post Office onto the Cornhill. A line of cars was parked along the pavement, reminding us of those long-ago days when we could drive into town and simply leave our car on the street where we wanted to go shopping! Parking restrictions were already in force around the town and eventually vehicles were banned completely from many of the streets around Ipswich town centre. The year 1951 was, of course, a rather special year, not just in Ipswich but around the country. Many readers will remember that the Festival of Britain, staged to celebrate the original Festival of 1851, was in full swing at the time. The Festival of Britain was the brain-child of Prince Albert, Queen Victoria's consort, and the extravaganza, which promoted British achievements, was staged in the purpose-built Crystal

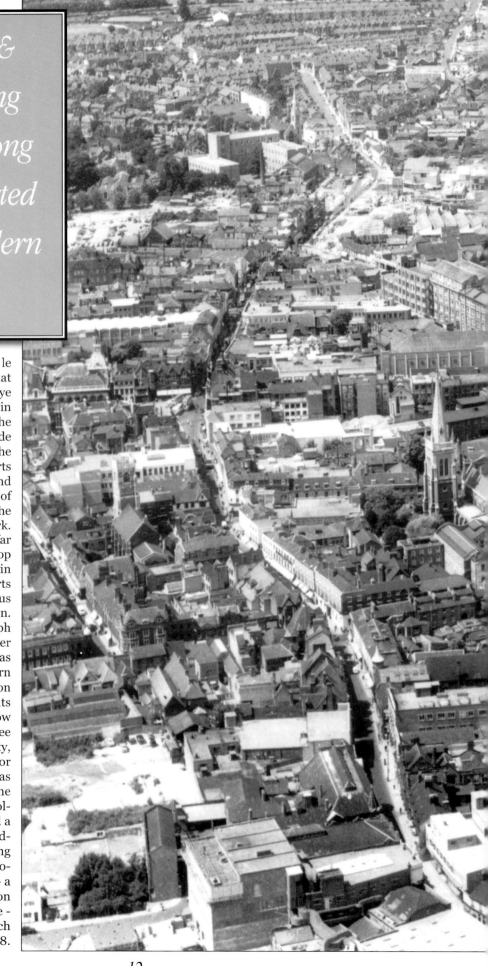

The Philips & Piper clothing factory has long gone - converted now into modern flats

The familiar spire of St Mary le Tower is the first landmark that draws the eye in this eagle's eye view of the town centre as it was in 1964 - a view that reminds us of the many changes that have been made in the town since then. Here, the appropriately solid Tower Ramparts school was still dispensing a sound education to the children of Ipswich, while the site across the road was being used as a car park. Today the land is put to a far different use, and we can shop indoors in warmth and comfort in the state of the art Tower Ramparts shopping centre, then catch a bus home from the nearby bus station. Towards the right of the photograph we can pick out the Philips & Piper clothing factory; the building was eventually converted into modern flats, and people are today living on the spot where we or our parents went to work each day. If we follow the line of Crown Street, we can see the premises of William Pretty, corsetiers, who were also major employers in the town. The area has changed completely, with the nearby residential housing demolished and replaced by offices and a car park. Nearby is the award-winning Crown Pools swimming complex. To the right of the photograph is Christchurch Park - a wonderful haven of peace right on the doorstep of the town centre - and its stately Tudor Christchurch Mansion, built in 1548.

Left: This fascinating bird's eye view takes us back to the Ipswich of the 1960s, when the new was rapidly emerging from the old. Princes Street cuts diagonally across from the bottom left of the photograph, and the night club that existed for a number of years under a variety of names can be seen in the centre of Princes Street round-about. A number of readers will remember the good nights out they had there in the days of their youth! The club's eventual demise was blamed largely on its central position, which meant either the crossing of busy roads or the risk of walking through the subways at night. The building has now been demolished. The building in the centre foreground is of course the Greyfriars development, which has itself changed quite drastically since this photograph was taken. The Greyfriars building was originally central to an ambitious plan to move the town's shopping area away from the old traditional shopping centre. Shops and a car park were provided, but most of the new units remained empty as the shoppers of Ipswich voted with their feet, preferring to stay with the old and familiar. Eventually the front part of the Greyfriars building was demolished to become an open forecourt, while the rest was converted to offices.
Civic Drive leads upwards from Princes Street roundabout, and a keen eye will spot the bare ribs of the spiral car park near the civic centre, still under construction.

Above: Little girl, big bags! Mum might be out of camera shot, but she would certainly have been nearby, probably herself loaded down with more bags, and Mum's little helper is determined to do her bit. We can only hope that the shopping trip was almost over and the two of them could head for home to rest their aching arms and tired feet. The little girl will very likely be a mother - and possibly a grandma - herself now; will she leaf through the pages of this book and recognise herself, we wonder, and remember those long-ago days when she and her mum used to go shopping together?
It was a sunny day on the Cornhill when they made their shopping trip, and we can see that railings on both sides of the road together with sets of traffic lights were doing their best to keep pedestrians and passing vehicles apart. Shopping here is thankfully far more of a pleasure today! A sharp eye will spot the ladder and scaffolding outside Lloyds Bank, though rather frustratingly for those who like to know what's going on, we are not able to see what work was in progress at the time. A 'No right turn' sign forbids drivers to turn into Lloyds Avenue, a street which did not exist before 1931.

Sporting life

Both pages: It was a proud moment for The Blues when with Scott Duncan as manager they won the Third Division South championship back in 1953-54 *(bottom)*. On the back row, left to right: W Reed, J Feeney, T Garneys, J Parry, G McLuckie, J Elsworthy, D Rees; front row: Scott Duncan, B Acres, A Crowe, T Parker, N Myles, T Brown and J Forsyth. Unfortunately, however, Town were to see the championship slip out of their grasp the following year....

By the 1956-57 season the talented Scott Duncan had departed - and a stroke of genius had brought Alf Ramsey to Town as manager. That season the Third Division South title was theirs once again, and at a reception at Ipswich Town Hall the triumphant side posed for the camera with their well-deserved shield *(below)*. Manager Alf Ramsey, as self effacing as ever, stands with the Mayor of Ipswich. Back row, left to right are Neil Myles, Billy Reed, Kenny Malcolm, and Leadbetter, while gathered around the shield in the front row stand Philips, Bailey, Elsworthy, Dai Rees, Tom Garneys and Basil Acres, with club director John Cobbold on the far right. Ipswich Town, described by many as

the 'Cinderella' of football, were not content to sit back and rest on their laurels, however; in 1960-61 they picked up the Second Division Championship. Further glory lay ahead the following season when with a 2-0 win against Aston Villa on April 28th the impossible happened and the 'underdog' clinched the league championship. The football world was left reeling and Alf Ramsey and his players found themselves in demand by the media *(facing page)* - as well as by their supporters, who went wild with joy and mobbed the victorious team. It was time to let the champagne corks pop!

Bottom: Watched by hundreds of supporters, a line of Witches' riders pause at the start of a race for the benefit of the photographer in an image that dates from the 1950s when speedway in Ipswich was still in its early days. The year 1951 saw the first challenge matches; Rayleigh was the very first fixture, though the 67-17 defeat was disappointing. After that, though, the only way was up, and excellent performances from bright young riders like Dick Shepherd, Harold McNaughton, Wal Morton, Sid Clark, Tich Read and Doug Papworth under track manager Arthur Franklin took the Witches through to the Southern League in 1952. The sport had rapidly become popular, and it was usual to see crowds of thousands turn out to cheer on their team at Foxhall. By 1953 quality riders such as Nobby Stock, Jimmy Grant, Bert Edwards and Len Silver were adding their input, and the team's position improved to third from the top from being third from the bottom. By the 1970s the Witches had established themselves as a team to be reckoned with, carrying off the British League title in 1975 and 1976, and the fabled John Louis, who had joined the side in 1970, came third in the 1975 world final at Wembley. Labelled the Witches' most successful rider, Louis went on to carry away trophy after trophy and title after title.

Right: Sir Alf was just plain Alf Ramsey when he was pictured behind his very basic desk at Portman Road. No sleek chrome and glass office with state-of-the-art technology and wall-to-wall carpeting for the great man; a desk, a phone - and his in-depth knowledge of football strategy were all the Ipswich manager needed to take his team from obscurity to the big time in five short years. Working on a shoestring budget, it was Alf's own genius for making shrewd signings and the individual talents and dedication of his players that put Ipswich Town on the map.

Born in 1922, Alf Ramsey first played for Dagenham, turning professional in the mid 1940s when he signed for Southampton. He later moved to Tottenham, where he spent his most successful playing years. In 1955 came a key move in his own career and in that of Ipswich - he was appointed as manager, guiding his team to victory in the Third, Second and First Division championships. As we all know, he went on to become England manager, bringing home the World Cup in 1966.

A quiet and reserved man by nature, Alf Ramsey was the master of understatement. His clipped English voice would be more likely to be heard telling someone that everyone had played very well than enthusing about how brilliant they were!

Loved by his players and well respected by everyone who came into contact with him, Sir Alf, as he became in 1967, was a figurehead in the realm of football. The soccer legend who was widely regarded as the finest manager in the world will continue to be sadly missed.

'Hail the champions!' and 'Well done, The Blues!' were phrases on everyone's lips as the town of Ipswich turned out to celebrate the triumph of Ipswich Town. It was Monday, 14th May 1962, and Town had just sent the soccer world spinning into shock by winning the First Division Championship.

The cheers of thousands of supporters filled the air as the team and officials took to their open-topped buses and toured the streets of Ipswich. Those who were there on that memorable day had seldom witnessed such a sight. As the parade progressed, some of the fans managed to walk alongside the

Continued overleaf

carpeted with humanity, with barely an inch to spare between the Town Hall and Lloyds Avenue. Echoing King Canute's fabled struggle against the incoming tide, lines of police officers linked arms to hold back the crowd and keep them from spilling into the roadway when the expected buses arrived bearing the triumphant team. What a day that must have been, not just for Town but for everyone who was part of the crowd - and that would surely have included many of our readers!

The history of Ipswich Town will forever in our minds be linked to players such as Dutch top shots Frans Thijssen and Arnold Muhren, who possessed a rare spark of genius that put the spotlight on Town in the late 1970s. And what about those unforgettable Ipswich legends Sir Alf Ramsey, responsible for England's triumph in tne 1966 World Cup, and player/manager Bobby Robson, who came within a hair's breadth of guiding England into the World Cup Final in 1990?

From previous page

coaches, keeping pace with their heroes, while others grabbed the best positions they could, crowding into upper windows to get a better view. The Cornhill, meanwhile, was wall to wall with ecstatic supporters and the entire square was

Wartime

Above: Ipswich Aerodrome was the setting for this photograph of workers from a centre where demobbed troops were given training. These ladies were key members of staff - and probably the most popular, as this was the catering team. Roast beef, vegetables, mashed potato and gravy, followed by jam roly-poly or treacle pudding and custard; just the job for a crew of hungry young blokes! The war was over, but its trappings were still dotted around the horizon, reminding everyone of the long dark tunnel of war they had just emerged from. A pill box can be made out in the distance, along with the airfield's fuel pumps. A forerunner of the airport was the Suffolk & East Counties Aeroplane Club, established in 1927 on a site between Ipswich and Hadleigh. The club saw lots of life in its early days, in fact in 1928 an incredible 5,000 people descended on the airfield for an air display. The crowd watched spellbound as an innovative plane with folding wings was unfolded and flown by one of the club's own pilots, Miss Sylvia Edwards, to demonstrate the possibilities of the unusual aircraft. Ipswich airport began life in 1930, and at first it was managed by the Aeroplane Club. The airfield was not without its famous visitors; in June 1930 the Prince of Wales, who very briefly became Edward VIII, flew his own Westland Wapiti into Ipswich.

Right: 'She's the girl that makes the thing that drills the hole that holds the spring that drives the rod that turns the knob that works the thingamabob....' So went the popular wartime song that perfectly fits this situation at Ransomes Sims and Jefferies, where an overlooker demonstrates a process to a trainee. This far from domestic situation was caught on camera during the 1940s, when Britain's men were called into military service and women across the country found themselves doing the kind of job they had never done before. Many of them worked in engineering factories such as Ransomes, performing tasks that were usually looked on as 'jobs for the men'. Traditionally, British men have been regarded as the bread winners, going out to work every day to keep their wives and families. Their womenfolk saw to the children, shopped for food every day, made the meals, cleaned the house, and washed and ironed the family's clothes. Ransomes Sims and Jefferies were one of the mainstays of employment in Ipswich, keeping a large number of men and women in work. The huge engineering works, which at the time were near the dock in Orwell Works in Duke Street, are well known for their grass cutting machinery. They are less known perhaps as the producers of many of the vehicles for Ipswich's first trolley bus fleet.

Both pages: The war was over, and the people of Ipswich were tired of bombs, gas masks, the blackout and all the other privations of wartime Britain. When peace was declared after six long years of war they went wild with joy. Out came the bunting and the stepladders, and decorations were strung from house to house across every street, while patriotic Union Jacks were hung from bedroom windows to flap gaily in the breeze. Along with the rest of Britain Ipswich found the energy to let their hair down and organise Victory Parades, street parties, fireworks displays and bonfires. This happy party was held in Phoenix Road *(below left)* , where even the Christmas decorations were unpacked from their dusty box in the loft and pressed into service. Some of the ladies in this group look rather tired. They had the right to be - after all, they had done the very best they could through the dreary days of the war, making eggless cakes and carrot jam; turning the collars of their husbands' shirts; making do with their old clothes while their children wore hand-me-downs.

It was good to be alive when so many were not, and now it was party time; time to enjoy peace and look forward to a better future. The hated Adolph Hitler was present at the party held in Brunswick Road *(bottom)* and his effigy would no doubt be burnt later in the day. Revenge, it is said, is sweet - but vengeance was not theirs; Hitler had already renounced his dream of a thousand-year Reich and had gone ahead to meet his maker. He and Eva Braun had committed suicide together just the week before, on 30th April. In the Pacific the war continued for a further four months; the Japanese surrendered on September 13th.

Above: It was a lovely day for a party; the long war was over, the sun was shining, and these tots had a lot of living to do and hopefully a prosperous future to look forward to. Such deep thoughts were far from their minds, though, as the children gathered together at the Margaret Catchpole Hotel in Cliff Lane for their VE Day party in 1945. Closer to their thoughts were jelly and ice cream, cake and biscuits! Only the large coach built pram in the foreground indicates the decade; those wonderful prams were certainly well sprung and luxurious - but they must have taken up a considerable amount of space in every mother's living room!

When the war ended and the news that everybody was waiting for was announced, Ipswich, along with the rest of Britain, found the energy to let their hair down and organise parties in virtually every street across the town.

It was Britain's new Prime Minister, Clement Attlee, who brought the nation down from its euphoria with a resounding bump. He gave the country a serious warning that although Britain was once more at peace, there was no likelihood of prosperity for the country in the immediate future. Across the world countries were decimated by war, and there were worldwide food shortages. It would be several more years before people could stop using tinned dried eggs or shop for clothes without counting how many coupons they had.

Right: This view of army cadets waiting on Ipswich Station in 1963 takes us back in imagination to the dark days of war. The second world war had been over for many years; it was the cold war that was very much in the foreground of people's thoughts during the nervous days of the 1960s, when relations with the USSR were at sparking point. The great fear at the time was the possibility of World War III - a notion which in retrospect seems ridiculous but was the great talking-point of the day. War, however, was obviously very far from the thoughts of these lads, who were off to camp and were determined to enjoy themselves. The young guitarist would no doubt have been very popular, and his musical skills would have been much in demand. What song was he performing? We will never know. The cadets were being watched enviously by a local schoolboy, who was perhaps deciding that he would join the army himself when he was a little older. Meanwhile, he would find escape from his humdrum school life in the pages of his comic. How frustrating that we can't see what he was reading! Back in the 1960s he would have had plenty of choice....He could have been finding excitement in the adventures of the heroes in Victor or Hotspur; if his taste ran to humour rather than the edge-of-the-seat stuff he could have chosen the Beezer, the Dandy or the Beano. All favourites for many years.

The Queen's coronation gave not only Ipswich but every town in Britain an excuse to throw a country-wide party. Every town and village made their own plans to deck windows and doorways with red, white and blue garlands, hang bunting across every street, run up the Union Jack from every flagpole and plan street parties for all the local kids. Dances were held, shows were staged, fireworks displays were put on and new songs were composed to celebrate the occasion - perhaps readers will remember 'Let's all be new Elizabethans'? Ipswich held a carnival that turned out to be one of those rare, never to be forgotten events that will stay with us for life. How many little boys (and big ones too!) would have been thrilled at the sight of this beautiful replica of the Golden Hind that formed one of the carnival floats, and the jolly pirates that accompanied it! Hundreds gathered along Tavern Street to watch the parade pass by to the foot-tapping rhythm of the band. Though television aerials were few and far between on the chimneys of Ipswich, perhaps a few people among this crowd would have been able to watch the crowning of the Queen in Westminster Abbey on television; it was the very first time the coronation of a British monarch had been filmed.

Events & occasions

Below: The pageantry of the Queen's coronation in June 1953 was echoed in the streets of Ipswich, who decided to stage an ambitious carnival to mark the event. Many of our readers will have been among the crowd that day, if not privileged to have been taking part in the proceedings. Thousands of people lined the route of the procession, and children crowded to the front or were lifted up by Mum or Dad to marvel at the intricate costumes and ingenious tableaux that had been put together by the organisers, who would have been working on the costumes and props for weeks if not months beforehand. Each float was themed; the Witches had a tableau of their own,

manned by one of the team's riders and his bike; others, like this one, had a nautical flavour. This ingenious tableau of mermaids swimming in the sea, and the Statue of Liberty standing on a raised dais, emphasised our links with the USA. By 1953 the grey days of wartime austerity were behind us, but post-war prosperity had some way to go before the nation could really relax. The coronation gave everyone a reason to throw a party, and the flags, bunting and banners that had been carefully packed away after the end of the war were hunted up and given another airing. There was scarcely a street in the town without its banners of red white and blue.

A glance at the 1940s

HOT OFF THE PRESS

At the end of World War II in 1945 the Allies had their first sight of the unspeakable horrors of the Nazi extermination camps they had only heard of until then. In January, 4,000 emaciated prisoners more dead than alive were liberated by the Russians from Auschwitz in Poland, where three million people, most of them Jews,were murdered. The following year 23 prominent Nazis faced justice at Nuremberg; 12 of them were sentenced to death for crimes against humanity.

THE WORLD AT LARGE

The desert area of Alamogordo in New Mexico was the scene of the first atomic bomb detonation on July 16, 1945. With an explosive power equal to more than 15,000 tons of TNT, the flash could be seen 180 miles away. President Truman judged that the bomb could secure victory over Japan with far less loss of US lives than a conventional invasion, and on 6th August the first of the new weapons was dropped on Hiroshima. Around 80,000 people died.

ROYAL WATCH

By the end of World War II, the 19-year-old Princess Elizabeth and her distant cousin Lieutenant Philip Mountbatten RN were already in love. The King and Queen approved of Elizabeth's choice of husband, though they realised that she was rather young and had not mixed with many other young men. The engagement announcement was postponed until the Princess had spent four months on tour in Africa. The couple's wedding on 20th November 1947 was a glittering occasion - the first royal pageantry since before the war.

The sight of this pair of magnificent horses and dray outside The Selkirk have attracted a large number of children (and their parents too!). Naturally enough, the horses with their ornamental brasses are attracting more looks than the representatives aboard the dray, though they too look very dashing in their bowler hats and smart outfits. The date was August 1958 - a warm and pleasant day - and the promotion had been organised by brewers Steward & Patterson Ltd

(who were later taken over by the giants Courage). Few among the crowd have noticed the photographer and his camera, and the result is this charming and natural scene. A number of the children have bikes of their own (note the one in the foreground sporting a genuine wicker basket); but spot the child across the road riding on his scooter! How long is it since you saw a child riding a scooter? These simple two-wheeled toys seem to have died a death in recent years, supplanted by roller blades and skateboards. But weren't they good fun? In the 1940s and 50s there were few children who were without a scooter. So many of the old toys and pastimes have disappeared almost without our noticing; do you remember magic painting books, whips and tops, and paper dolls with their paper clothes? All departed one by one.

The Household Cavalry have just disembarked from their train, and a large crowd of onlookers has turned out to watch the procession of beautiful animals leave Ipswich Station. The event is believed to have been part of the coronation celebrations that were held in the town in 1953; the 'holiday runabout' tickets advertised near the station entrance help us to date the photograph.

The coronation was a red letter day in the diary of everyone in town. Not only were there the official events such as the carnival parade to look forward to, but there were the many street parties, dances and fireworks parties to enjoy. The coronation itself is well-remembered by a nation who saw it on television; for many people it was the first time they had ever watched TV - a difficult concept for us to grasp so many years on, when we are used to being surrounded by technology of all kinds. But for those who were privileged to be among those early viewers, the sight was one they will never forget. The new queen being anointed with oil and having the crown placed upon her head, then riding happily back to the palace in her golden coach, wearing the crown and carrying the orb and sceptre, is a precious memory.

Above: *The date of this photograph is well recorded - it was 2nd June 1953 when this group of senior citizens gathered to watch the Queen's coronation on television. The weather was cool for the time of year and persistent drizzle put a damper on many parties across Britain; judging by the number of coats and hats in the photograph, it was chilly indoors as well as out! These were the people who had supported their country through two world wars. They had seen the marvellous work done by King George VI and Queen Elizabeth during the World War II, and now the King had passed on they were determined to welcome his beautiful daughter to the throne. Television was a novelty to the vast majority of people at the time. Although Britain had a television service as early as 1936 (suspended during the second world war), few people could afford to buy the expensive sets - and the range of programmes was very limited anyway. Another drawback was the size of the TV screens; many early sets had tiny screens, and a lot of viewers bought specially-made magnifying glasses which fitted over the front of the front of the set and made viewing more comfortable.*

By the 1950s sets were beginning to get cheaper, and the Queen's Coronation presented many families with the ideal reason to buy or rent a TV set. Those who did not simply crowded into the parlours of more fortunate neighbours to watch the event!

Above: Decorations, party hats, sandwiches, cakes and jelly - all the ingredients that go into giving the children a good time were there when this community in Beck Street threw a party to celebrate the Queen's coronation. The day was cool, but what of it? All that was needed was a warm coat and perhaps a headscarf or cap.... The games and races, and perhaps dancing for the grown-ups, would come later. It was the same story everywhere, as Ipswich geared up into party mood.

The coronation came a mere eight years after the end of World War Two, and people felt that they could relax for the first time. Across Britain, each town and city, every village institute and church, took the opportunity to declare their loyalty to the new Queen, and each held their own event, ranging from a simple street party to a big parade. In Ipswich, flags flew from every available window, garlands and banners were hung in windows, lines of bunting stretched across every street, and every major building in the town had its artistic decoration.

The celebrations left few people in Ipswich without a precious collection of happy memories to look back on and treasure. The news on the morning of the coronation carried other news that the world had been waiting for - Edmund Hillary, with John Hunt and Sherpa Tensing, had reached the summit of Everest. The Daily Express headline said it all: 'All this and Everest Too'!

Below: The declaration of Queen Elizabeth II's accession to the throne was a solemn occasion, and representatives from the RAF, the army and the navy gathered with a large crowd in front of the Town Hall to hear the official proclamation. Their joy was tinged with sadness, of course, for the Queen's father, King George VI, was genuinely mourned by the whole nation. Many were in tears when they heard of his death. A heavy smoker for many years, King George had begun to suffer poor health in 1948, when he developed circulation problems, and in the early 1950s he was found to be suffering from lung cancer. On 30th January 1952 he and the Queen went to the airport to see Princess Elizabeth and Prince Philip off on their African tour. The couple were never to see him again; he died in his sleep on 5th February. Unlike her father King George VI, the young and pretty new queen had begun her training for the throne early, when Edward VIII's abdication in 1936 made her the heir presumptive to the throne. She was only 14 years old when she broadcast messages of encouragement to the children of war-torn Britain, and as the war progressed she gradually took on more and more public duties.

This page: It was July 1961, and the Queen was coming to town - a good excuse, if one was needed, to freshen up the paintwork and let Her Majesty know that Ipswich had gone to the trouble to make her feel welcome. Out came the ladders, the overalls and the paintbrushes, and all the traders along the route that the royal procession would take set aside a few hours to smarten up their property. The route included Fore Street, and we can see from this photograph that when these painters got busy the decorations, in the form of colourful garlands, were already in place. Every retailer had painstakingly cleaned windows, hung up hanging baskets of flowers and done anything else they could think of to make her visit a memorable one. The purpose of the royal visit was the official opening of the new Civic College, where the Queen unveiled a smart plaque. The college was to eventually become the University College of Suffolk.

Thousands of cheering people lined the route of the royal procession, taking advantage of every upper window to get a better view. Children threaded their way through to the front to get a roadside position - a spot which had the added bonus of temporary railings with a nice handy rail that could be climbed upon. Her Majesty's limousine is here crossing from Fore Street into Upper Orwell Street *(below),* and Martin & Newby, looking much the same then as now, was looking particularly smart on that special day in its sparkling paint and cheerful decorations.

Martin & Newby have long been regarded as *the* place to buy hardware and ironmongery; anything from gardening tools to brass screws and from electric table lamps to door handles could be purchased there. Keen DIYers have learned through experience to make Martin & Newby their first port of call instead of the last, especially when searching for those elusive bits and pieces that sometimes are so hard to find!

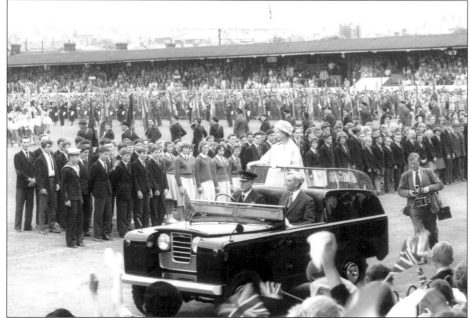

Both pages: A right royal welcome to Her Majesty! Ipswich is a riot of red, white and blue; patriotic flags fly from the Town Hall, children wave their union jacks enthusiastically, and crowds of thousands line the route to cheer themselves hoarse as the Queen's black limousine glides silently from Princes Street into Tavern Street. The date was 21st July 1961 - the day Queen Elizabeth II visited Ipswich, and it was of great importance to everyone to obtain the best view possible of Her Majesty as she was driven around the town. Old and young alike began to gather well beforehand; if they were lucky they might receive a warm and friendly smile and that characteristic stately wave as the Queen went by in her shining black Rolls Royce, its royal insignia proclaiming its illustrious occupant.

Thousands more gathered at Portman Road, where the Queen was to meet a number of dignitaries and VIPs. Weeks before the occasion, Girl Guides and Scouts had painstakingly gone through their positions in the line-up; bands had carefully rehearsed their rousing marches, and every association and organisation had practised their own part in the proceedings. The preparations having been made, at long last the day that everyone had been waiting for arrived. The dry weather was a bonus, and she was able to stand in her customised open-topped Land Rover as it slowly As the Queen circuited Portman Road; the envied youngsters who were able to line up for a ringside view counted themselves very lucky to see their smiling Queen in close-up.

The face that launched a thousand stylophones! Can't you just hear Rolf Harris asking these children, 'Can you see what it is yet?' In this case, it was the star's signature in the autograph books of his young fans! Many of our readers will remember these immortal words from their childhood, however, taking a trip down memory lane to the days when they sat wide-eyed in front of the television to watch Rolf Harris's Cartoon Time. It is many years since the versatile Australian proved himself to be a gifted cartoonist, drawing pictures line by line with a confident hand while he talked animatedly to his young viewers, who were meant to guess the subject of his picture.

These excited young fans had caught up with Rolf (looking a tad younger then) during a visit to the Ambassador Bowling Alley in July 1963, and judging by the broad smiles on their faces, Rolf was exchanging some entertaining banter with the children. Today's viewers have become used to seeing this obviously caring man on Animal Hospital that they forget (or perhaps the younger ones never knew?) about those hit records he used to make. But fondly remembered by those of us who were young-sters at the time are songs such as 'Two Little Boys' and 'Jake the Peg'. And who can forget 'Stairway to Heaven'? Great stuff.

and-a-half acre site in Colchester Road was chosen, and work on the much-needed new fire station began. The new building was opened by the Mayor of Ipswich, Alderman A V Bishop, and the staff moved in on 4th November 1962 - complete with a half-cooked lunch; the cooking was finished in the new kitchens!

Above: When a small fire started at Haddock and Baines in Princes Street back in February 1950, it quickly spread, fuelled by the paper and inks stored on the premises of this printing firm and paper merchants. The building was soon well alight and the fire brigade was called as the blaze became a roaring inferno which spread to the adjoining Central cinema on one side, and printers T G Garrod Ltd on the other. The photograph shows the buildings at the height of the blaze, the flames reflecting eerily in the puddles on the road. The fire was a difficult one to tackle, as the equipment in use by the fire brigade was old fashioned, its trailer pumps and tenders dating back to the second world war. There was little left when the fire was eventually extinguished and the damage was estimated at £100,000. At the time the fire brigade was operating from premises that had become insufficient to meet the needs of a modern service, and the accommodation, much of which was in prefabricated buildings, fell below the required standards. A two-

Top: A pause in the proceedings at Broom Hill open air swimming pool gives the spectators, staff, parents and swimmers alike a few minutes' breathing space. It was the Ipswich inter-schools events of June 1965, and the competitive feeling was high as each school cheered on their own side in the 100 metre relay, the diving events, the butterfly, breast-stroke, back-stroke - and all the other races, both team and individual. A good crowd had turned out that day, and the weather, judging by the jackets, blazers and even scarves worn by the spectators, could possibly have been rather cool for the time of year - though perhaps the scarves were worn more as support for the children's own school colours rather than as a way of keeping out a chilly wind. Swimming has for many years figured high in the popularity stakes among Ipswich schools, along with athletics events and team sports like the ever favoured soccer. Broom Hill swimming pool, however, was more than just a place to hold school galas. On hot summer days in the long school holidays the open air facility was the ideal way to cool off; the problem, of course, was the frequency of *cool* summer days. Even in quite pleasant weather you would often find more people sitting around the water than swimming in it!

Mason's paper, available all hours

During the mid-19th century, Mr Mason moved to Ipswich from the Midlands. The circumstances surrounding his move are scantily documented; it is thought that he came from Leicestershire, but little is known about his former life or the reasons behind his decision to come to live in Ipswich. However, what is certain is that he and his family settled here; and in due course his son Oswald Mason set up as a paper maker in the village of Bramford, on the outskirts of Ipswich.

Unfortunately Oswald's mill in Paper Mill Lane, Bramford, was not ideally sited for paper manufacture. Paper is normally made from wood pulp - although over the years it has also been made from straw, from plant materials such as the Egyptian papyrus which has given paper its name, and from a mixture of cloth rags traditionally used for the most expensive luxury papers. Originally these raw materials were soaked and rendered into a paste-like slurry, then spread over fabric-covered frames to allow the excess water to drain away. Later when the sheets of paper had dried out they were peeled off the fabric screen (- interestingly, the tradition of the 'water mark' which still serves today to identify different brands of paper evolved from the marks left on the paper by the fabric screen on which it had dried. Nowadays 'water marks' are created with a raised symbol or logo being impressed into the wet pulp). Vast quantities of clean, fresh water are essential for the various stages of paper-making process, whatever the raw material used; and the water supply to Oswald's mill was neither sufficiently plentiful nor sufficiently pure to produce anything other than low-grade brown wrapping paper. This was a major problem as it severely limited the development potential of the business, and it soon became clear that the mill could never be a great success. Oswald persevered in manufacturing brown paper for a while, then turned instead to paper distribution and became an agent for kraft papers and wrapping papers to a limited list of customers.

Meanwhile, Mr Mason's other son had established Mason's Cement Works at Claydon. Cement from Mason's Cement Works found many uses, from farm labourer's cottages to the industrial installations erected by the railway and port companies, often on a monumental scale

and often, too, very pleasing to the eye. Having left its mark on the architecture of Suffolk, Mason's Cement Works was long ago taken over by the famous Blue Circle Cement Company.

After successfully guiding his company through the fiercely rationed years of the second world war, Oswald Mason died suddenly, while under the barber's towel

Above: *Peter Kenny, chairman of the company, who entered the business in 1956.*
Right: *Mason's Friars Road premises in 1962.*

during his regular visit to his local barber, leaving Mason's Paper Mill Company to his daughter Pamela. However, Pamela Mason was not in position to devote herself completely to the running of her father's old business, which sadly went into decline. In the 1950s Mason's Paper Mill Company had an annual turnover of £11,000, which, even in the 1950s when professional men lived comfortably on around £1,000 a year, was somewhat low for a commercial firm.

One of Pamela Mason's regular customers was Burton Son and Sanders, a firm of wholesale bakery suppliers who bought their wrapping papers from Mason's. Pamela's contact there was Ian B Liddell, a shrewd, energetic man with a keen business sense. From his conversations with Pamela each time she called upon him, Mr Liddell realised that Mason's was struggling, and he saw an excellent opportunity of acquiring the business with it's potential for growth. This, in effect, was what happened. Ian Liddell bought into Mason's and left Burton Son and Sanders' employ to set about developing his new business interest. This was renamed The Mason's Paper Company, subsequently becoming The Mason's Paper Company Limited in 1955.

As part of his development strategy, Ian Liddell acquired Sproughton Mill which provided extensive, low-cost warehousing space for the paper bags and the greaseproof and imitation greaseproof papers which the firm supplied to butchers, fishmongers and greengrocers; there was a constant demand for cheap bags and wrapping papers which shopkeepers used, so to maximise on the business it was necessary to stock in volume. In addition to the warehouse Ian Liddell rented a one room office, all of ten feet square with one desk, on the top floor of an office block in Princess Street, Ipswich.

In the 1950s a revolution in shopping habits began. Before then it was normal, even essential for a full-time housewife who had no freezer to shop daily for fresh produce and perishable goods which were difficult to keep, even after they had been cooked. Remember when sugar and dried fruit were bagged to order? And butter, like cheese, was cut, patted and wrapped to your request as you waited? These comfortable habits which allowed many housewives the opportunity to meet similarly-engaged friends for morning tea (coffee was a rare luxury then) and a gossip, were brought to an end by jobs for the girls. The working woman's routine was aided by the introduction in the 1950s of 'self-service' shops, and many long-established grocers followed the trend, ripping out their counters and replacing them with racks and aisles and cash checkouts. Some people still miss the days when the 'customer was queen', and have never mentally adjusted to shops where the customer does all the work and pays for the privilege! Since those early days, self-service shops have given way in their turn to supermarkets, and paper bags have now been almost totally replaced by polythene wrappers and those difficult-to-open plastic bags.

20 - enjoyed the convenience of having warehouse and office facilities under one roof. This was the first of three moves made by the rapidly expanding company. Over the next ten years the firm continued to grow as printers struggled to keep up with the increasing demand created by the commercial and public sectors for brochures, letterheads and other printed material.

The majority of printers operate on a day-by-day basis, catering for customers who regularly want work completed as soon as possible, if not sooner. The printing industry cannot afford to delay jobs while they wait for materials, but neither can they afford to tie up capital, let alone space, in holding large stocks of papers; and indeed they have no need to do so, when instead they can rely on paper wholesalers such as Mason's, who can quickly supply any grade and colour of paper that a customer might choose. Printers operating to tight schedules must be confident of obtaining the right goods at the right time from their supplier, and over the years Mason's has built up excellent relationships with its customers throughout East Anglia and into London through giving consistently reliable and efficient service.

1977, the Queen's Jubilee Year, saw Masons move to their current premises near the Ransomes factory. Ransomes, who became famous as manufacturers of patent agricultural machinery and lawnmowers, had undertaken the development of a large area of land around their factory for industrial use, creating the industrial estate now known as the Ransomes Europark.

The 1980s saw Mason's well established as East Anglia's leading supplier of papers to the printing trade and looking to the future with confidence, with paper-bags and greaseproof wrappings consigned forever to the company's history books. Ian Liddell, the then Chairman, retired in 1986. Malcolm Lane-Ley, the current MD, took

The knock-on effect of these changes was foreseen by Ian Liddell and Peter Kenny. Peter had joined the business in 1956 and three years later, in 1959, Ian decided to invest in a small range of white bond printing paper as a supplement to the wrapping papers which he stocked. In the same year the business moved its administrative department from its single-room company headquarters to a converted house in Friars Road, as by then the firm was employing a total staff of six at both sites. At this point they set themselves what seemed like an ambitious target: to reach a £1million annual turnover. In fact this was achieved by the late 1960s - representing an impressive rate of growth over just one decade.

During the 'Swinging Sixties' the Mason's Paper Company moved from its two existing premises to a single site in Duke Street, where the staff - by now numbering around

Above: *The Duke Street premises.*
Above left: *Sproughton Mill, the company's first warehouse in the 1950s.*

the post over in 1997, and Peter Kenny is currently Chairman, having been MD for many years previously.

During 1984 Mason's was acquired by Bunzl plc so that, as part of a large group, its position at the leading edge of paper suppliers to the print industry was assured. From this stage Bunzl formed their Fine Paper Division, of which Mason's is an autonomous unit, enjoying the benefits of large-scale national purchasing through Bunzl Fine Paper. The range of stock covers an extensive selection of weights (measured in grams) and thicknesses (measured in microns) of different papers for different purposes. And, with the glorious range of colours and

textures which are available, it is easy to see how working with such a stock is fascinating and enjoyable.

The opening of two more branches of Mason's during the 1980s allowed the firm to expand its markets further afield. One branch was opened in Cambridge in the early 80s to cover the surrounding counties, followed by the Hornchurch branch in the mid-80s which supplies the London area. This effectively gives complete coverage of the triangle formed by London and East Anglia. Regular overnight deliveries from Ipswich to each branch ensure that stock levels are always maintained, ready for delivery. The present Ipswich warehouses have a total storage area

of 55,000 square feet, and can easily hold hundreds of tonnes of paper which are always kept in stock.

As well as books, much of Mason's paper is destined for business use, both for advertising and promotional material and for business stationery - which includes not only letterheads, compliment slips and the paper on which annual reports and accounts are printed, but also transactional print using carbonless paper for multiple copies of such documents as invoices and statements. Companies are becoming increasingly aware of the extent to which their corporate image can be enhanced and reinforced by making sure that all their documentation, not just their

correspondence, is issued on consistently good quality paper. For advertising, textured paper is often selected for greater impact; Mason's range of textured papers offers an excellent choice for those prepared to spend a little more in order to make a strong mental impression on readers. Even the simplest and cheapest of booklets such as parish magazines and monochrome (single colour) leaflets can be visually enhanced by selecting a single colour paper.

Above: *This fascinating view of Ipswich and her docks, an essential part of the life of the town, was taken from the gasometer some years ago.*

In fact, the overall impression given by any document is influenced to some extent by the paper it is printed on; next time you study a business report or a tourist flier you will understand the power of colour and texture in influencing human senses and intellect.

This simple psychology is well understood by the printers who can give their customers valuable advice on choosing a paper, and then, when the decision has been made, turn to Mason's to supply it. Mason's is also aware of the psychology of keeping customers happy, which in their case means providing a sound product and a first rate service to ensure repeat business. By maintaining such a large and varied stock of papers, Mason's is able to offer a 24-hour delivery service; a surprisingly large proportion of orders reach customers on the day they were placed, and the rest arrive the following day.

To meet the needs of those customers who work out of normal office hours in order to complete specific jobs or special orders, members of Mason's warehouse team are on call at weekends and during public holidays. Whether the customer needs expert advice or materials, Mason's is on hand to provide whatever assistance is required, immediately.

In addition to conventional papers, printers also require reels and sheets for the latest technology, digital printing, both of which Mason's can supply. A number of printers place orders with Mason's several times a day, passing on

orders as they receive them from their customers. These can be for low or high volume work, ranging from a special card for a few hundred invitations to paper and card for several thousand twenty-page booklets. Businesses often have unexpected runs on their brochures and stationery which then need replenishing in a hurry, and when this happens their printers turn to Masons, confident that the material they need will not only be in stock but delivered without delay.

Right: *Mr Ian Liddell at his retirement function in 1986 pictured with his wife Mary and their three daughters.*
Below: *The Sales Office staff in the mid 1990s.*

Delivery is carried out by the Operations Department, which maintains a fleet of 30 delivery vans and lorries, many equipped with tail-lifts. Although a single sheet of paper is light enough to flutter in a breeze, paper becomes incredibly dense, solid and weighty when stacked in reams and boxes. Anyone who has ever tried to lift a sizeable box of books, an office's monthly stationery delivery or even a large pile of newsprint will know that considerable strength is required, and the correct lifting technique should always be employed in order to avoid injury. However, paper, for all its weight and solidity, must be handled gently as it can be easily damaged in transit, rendering it unfit for passing through modern high-speed printing presses, some of which can run at speeds in excess of 10,000 sheets an hour. Even the humblest of office photocopiers has a way of protesting at the slightest irregularity that mars the smoothness of paper which passes between its rollers, as every secretary will know! Printing papers are wrapped by the ream (500 sheets) in a water-repellant or waterproof-grade paper; the ubiquitous A4, for instance, is then packed five reams to the box. Typically, a load consists of a number of pallets of various packets of papers which have been carefully assembled by forklift. All delivery vehicles are equipped with modern communications so that the driver can keep in radio contact with Head Office in Ipswich, with the Cambridge and Hornchurch branches, and if needs be with the other drivers as well. Even the most scrupulously-maintained vehicles are not immune to the occasional mechanical breakdown or mishap, but by taking prompt action to make alternative arrangements, usually by sending out another vehicle, and by keeping the customer informed of the progress of their order, the delivery team's reputation for complete reliability and trustworthiness is kept unblemished.

The responsibility for ensuring that all goes smoothly in this Department lies with Barry Kent, Operations Director. Barry has been with the company for more than 30 years, ever since he left school. The firm's policy of internal promotion, together with the very good working conditions which all its staff enjoy, has led to Mason's becoming known locally as an excellent employer, and so even in an area where there is no shortage of work Mason's is able to retain a stable workforce with a high percentage of long-serving staff.

The loyalty and the positive contribution of all Mason's employees are important factors in the success of the entire operation, which depends upon real team work between the different departments. As in any business, the firm's reputation depends not just on the goods supplied but on human contacts with those who make it possible. We all know how important first impressions are. Often it is the outside sales representatives, under Sales Director Alastair Nash, who are the new customer's first contact with the firm. But the ability and willingness to help customers solve their problems by staying polite, confident, efficient and helpful even in a crisis is noticeable at every level throughout this company. The smartly-uniformed delivery men, in clean well-maintained vehicles, are also salesmen by virtue of their contact with customers, a policy which some companies neglect - to their cost. Beyond the visible tip of the iceberg lies a well-ordered structure of human, mechanical and technological systems which keeps Mason's Paper operating smoothly. Good leadership and co-operation at all levels provides the ambience in which individuals work together to achieve individual and corporate success.

Above: *The modern day premises at Ransomes Europark, to where the company moved in 1977 and subsequently acquired two further units.*

At leisure

Below: It was 1955; the circus was coming to town, and crowds were gathering for a free show as the elephants - surely the strangest passengers that Ipswich station had ever seen - took to the road to walk to the circus ground. In this case it was more likely to have been the corner of Ranelagh Road and London Road (within easy walking distance from the station) than Christchurch Park. This might have been a free show, but many of these curious onlookers would shortly have been dipping into their pockets to see the show as the exciting roll of the drums drew them and their families to Chipperfields Circus. Full of life and colour and the smell of sawdust, the circus was a major attraction, especially to children. The antics of the clowns playing pranks on each other - and on members of the audience - had them roaring with laughter, while the high wire act and the graceful trapeze artists kept them on the edge of their seats. Will the performer lose his balance and slip off the tightrope in front of our eyes? Will the trapeze artist, dressed in her colourful spangled costume, miss the outstretched hands of her partner? All very thrilling stuff, and calculated to send any child home tired and satisfied at the end of a wonderful afternoon or evening out.

Right: This cosy scene at the Queen's Head in St Matthews Street puts us in mind of the pub that TV viewers all around the country know as well as their own local - the Rover's Return. This time, however, nobody would be returning.... The Queen's Head had become a part of life for local residents, who had been used to popping in on the odd evening during the week and had certainly spent most Saturday

evenings chatting to friends - and downing a pint or three of their favourite brew. But the camera has caught for the record a moment of history - the landlord pulling what was probably the historical last pint in the pub that had been a favourite for many years. The geography of Ipswich was about to change, and a large number of properties along St Matthews Street were on the planners' hit list as the town was given the dual carriageway that it so badly needed. It was New Year's Eve, making it easier for the regulars who crowded into the pub for the last time to look cheerful; the pub's last night could have turned into a far more sober occasion. Even the landlord and his lady look remarkably cheerful. Could they have been about to jet off to Spain for a well-earned holiday? Or were they retiring and simply looking forward to taking life easy in their future years? Sadly, we will never know....

This tranquil scene of the Wet Dock was captured in 1955, and two barges - the front one heavily laden - sail out of the lock gates. The Wet Dock was constructed in 1842, the brain child of Henry Palmer. The docks form part of the rich history of the port of Ipswich, and in earlier years their maltings, grain terminals, mills, factories, warehouses and public houses bustled with life. This part of town was once a lively community of homes, shops, pubs and churches, where life revolved around the employment offered by the sea and its related industries. Little remains, however, of industries such as grain, animal feed, coal and fertiliser, once closely linked to the docks area. Ransomes, Sims & Jefferies Ltd operated from the Orwell works, closed down in 1968; Ransomes and Rapier Ltd operated from the Waterside Works on Griffin Wharf, closed in 1988, and the town's gasworks ceased its operations in 1970. Fortunately many of the original buildings - some of them incredibly dating back to the 17th century - still stand as a reminder of the thriving docks community, though in many cases their use has changed more than a little.

On the move

Above: The Tower Ramparts area has changed beyond recognition since this view was captured back in August 1956, the only similarity being the provision of public transport! The 'green' bus station has of course replaced this well-filled car park. A number of cars can be seen heading towards the exit; they don't appear to have left any empty spaces behind them, however, so perhaps their drivers are touring the town, looking for a place to leave the car while they nip off to do an hour or so's shopping. This was 1956, and the family car was now within the reach of the ordinary person in the street. Post-war prosperity had at last become a reality to many families, some of whom had more than one wage coming into the household. The second world war had taken women into the workplace, and when peace was declared in 1945 many of them were reluctant to give up their new-found freedom. At last they could purchase the kind of luxuries that their mothers had to get along without - washing machines, modern cookers, electric irons, kettles and vacuum cleaners. Housework was no longer the chore it had traditionally been, and women were anxious to shed their aprons and get out into the workplace. If the ladies in this photograph could have seen into the future they would have marvelled at the Tower Ramparts shopping centre that one day would replace the old secondary school.

Below: Now where's the nearest car park...? The driver of this rather splendid Morris 12 saloon is obviously slightly fazed by the fact that his usual car park in Lady Lane has been closed down. Directing motorists to a free alternative car park at Portmans Walk seems to have been part of this police officer's duties. The well-polished Morris and Rover - both black, of course, reflecting the predominant colour of the day - give us a pleasant trip back in time; they could both have possibly been around 20 years old when the photograph was taken in 1964. They present us with an interesting contrast between the somewhat austere lines that were typical of earlier decades, and the lighter, more rounded lines of the Morris Minor and the Singer that creep into the background. The popular Morris Minor was designed by Alexander Issigonis (who was also responsible for giving us the mini) - an example of mono-coque construction, which had no separate chassis. Interestingly the Morris Minor was the first all-British car to sell more than one million. Most of these houses in Lady Lane, which connected Elm Street with Hyde park Corner, were earmarked for demolition in the town's redevelopment scheme that changed so much of our scenery.

Snapped in the early 1950s, a single deck motor bus heads off towards Queen Street between the Post Office and the Town Hall. Buses have long been looked on as convenient mobile advertising hoardings; this one advertises the locally brewed Cobbolds beer. Cobbolds have been brewing in Ipswich since 1746, and it would be just a few years after this photograph was taken that Cobbolds merged with the rival firm Tollemache, who were themselves one of the biggest brewers in Ipswich. The bus was closely followed by a motor cyclist - and readers will immediately spot the fact that he is not wearing a helmet. Far less emphasis was placed on safety issues back then; legislation on the wearing of protective motor cycle gear and safety clothing for workers still lay in the future.

Even in ancient times the Cornhill was at the heart of the town's life, and markets, fairs, meetings and

A glance at the 1950s

WHAT'S ON?

Television hit Britain in a big way during the 1950s. Older readers will surely remember Double Your Money, Dixon of Dock Green and 'Dragnet' (whose characters' names were changed 'to protect the innocent').
Commercial television was introduced on 22nd September 1955, and Gibbs SR toothpaste were drawn out of the hat to become the first advert to be shown. Many believed adverts to be vulgar, however, and audiences were far less than had been hoped for.

GETTING AROUND

The year 1959 saw the development of the world's first practical air-cushion vehicle - better known to us as the hovercraft. The earliest model was only able to travel at slow speeds over very calm water and was unable to carry more than three passengers. The faster and smoother alternative to the sea ferry quickly caught on, and by the 1970s a 170-ton car-carrying hovercraft service had been introduced across the English Channel.

SPORTING CHANCE

The four-minute mile had remained the record since 1945, and had become regarded as virtually unbreakable. On 6th May 1954, however, Oxford University student Roger Bannister literally ran away with the record, accomplishing the seemingly impossible in three minutes 59.4 seconds. Bannister collapsed at the end of his last amazing lap, even temporarily losing his vision. By the end of the day, however, he had recovered sufficiently to celebrate his achievement in a London night club!

ceremonies were regularly held there. The town's stocks and pillory also stood there, and those unfortunates sentenced to a few hours' punishment - deserved or not - would suffer the taunts (and possibly the odd bad egg or two) of the market shoppers. To them, it was all part of the day's entertainment, though perhaps not so entertaining to the recipients! The more town's more gruesome history is also linked with this spot, as nine people were burned at the stake under the reigns of Henry VIII and his daughter, dubbed 'Bloody Mary'.

Above: 'Now how did this thing go...?' Two young women watch this conductor as he gets used to his new machine, and it looks as though a certain amount of light-hearted banter is being exchanged. (Did it also involve the exchange of telephone numbers, we wonder?)

The new ticket machines, introduced to Ipswich buses on 30th August 1951, required the bus conductors to think before they pressed the levers, at least until they got used to them. Soon, however, operating the new 'Ultimate' ticket machines would come naturally. Tickets were re-printed with the prices, and all the conductor needed to do was set the fare stage, stamp and press, and Bob's your uncle, out pops the ticket. The new system replaced the old machines that used a roll of white paper. Using a dial like that of a telephone, the relevant information was stamped on to the paper and the ticket torn off. Trams were inclined to use yet another system - the 'Bell Punch' machine - that resembled a mouse trap. The machine held racks of pre-printed tickets in which the conductor punched a hole in the appropriate fare stage. All of which, of course, meant little to the passenger, whose only interest was getting to work and back in the shortest possible time.

Above right: The *bad news* was that Ipswich was about to lose one of its well-used facilities; St Matthews car park in Lady Lane closed down on 28th September 1964. Only a small area was to remain in use, meaning that the majority of drivers would be left with the problem of having to find somewhere else to park. A helpful sign directed motorists to the car park in Portmans Walk opposite the corporation transport depot. The *good news* was that the alternative car park

was completely free! Older readers will remember the signs we could see dotted around our streets long ago - 'To Car FREE Park'; alas, free car parks remain a fond and far off memory! Even this one in Lady Street had its charges; the grand sum of ninepence (about four new pence) would secure you a parking place - though you could only stay there for twelve hours! Even in 1964, ninepence was hardly a swingeing charge. If you were a regular user of the car park and could afford to dig deep in your pocket, you could pay an annual fee of £8. So many years on, this sum seems quite ludicrous for a year's parking, where several pounds a day is the norm. We must remember, however, that £8 represented a weekly income back in the 1960s! St Matthews Street and the Lady Lane area were earmarked for huge changes that came with the redevelopments of the mid 1960s.

The vehicle in the background was very definitely the last trolley bus, and a sign fixed to the front of the bus rams the point home to any would-be passengers who were not aware of the fact. The bus that drove straight into the history books was on the Number 2 route to Priory Heath, and its final journey was from Tower Ramparts to the depot in Cobham Road. The quiet whirr of the trolley bus motor took over from the rattle of the tram back in the mid-1920s - and now it was the turn of the 'trackless trams', as they were widely known, to depart. Some of Ipswich's trolley buses were sold on to join the fleet of other towns such as Walsall, while the older and less fortunate ones were consigned to that great bus shed in the sky. Did this bus suffer the same fate of some 'last buses' in other towns, where souvenir hunters took away with them everything they could lay their hands on, even if it was nailed down? The crews' uniform jackets, destination blinds, headlamps and handrails were often carried away to moulder in lofts and attics around the country. The men who staffed this last bus got to record their names for posterity in the autograph books of the local children; how many of them survive, we wonder? Autograph hunting, once a craze that swept Britain, now seems to have died a natural death except perhaps in the case of film stars and rock bands!

We would all love to have been eavesdroppers on the confrontation between the drivers of these buses involved in a mishap on Bishops Hill, as one asks the other what the heck he's playing at (or words to that effect). It is thought that the trolley bus in front rolled into the single deck bus behind - but where the third vehicle fits in, we are not sure. We can see, however, that the big guys have the little guy well and truly boxed in! Trolley bus Number 113 (for enthusiasts, a Karrier F4 with a Park Royal body) is bound for Priory Heath on the Number 2 route, and its load of passengers gaze out of the window at the goings-on below, obviously hoping that all this would not take long,

Trolley-buses began to take over from trams in 1923

and they would quickly be on their way home again after a long day's work. Trolley buses began to take over from the trams in 1923, and their forward-thinking design included the use of one-man pay as you enter facilities, the first in the country. Their use was discontinued soon afterwards, however. Though the first vehicles were on hire from Rochester, the trolley buses proved to be such a success that the first of Ipswich Corporation's own fleet was ordered from Ransomes Sims and Jefferies. Trolley buses lived on in the town until 23rd August 1963, when the last vehicle, appropriately draped in black and labelled 'RIP', left for Priory Heath depot.

Shopping spree

How long is it since we saw traffic in Westgate Street? This photograph was taken in the late 1950s, when pedestrianisation was still a distant dream. The row of cycles parked along the kerb take us back in time and remind us of a gentler age, when we could park our bike outside a shop and expect them to be still there on our return! Remember Stones electrical shop? We can see from the sign above the window that they specialised in radio (still referred to as 'the wireless' by many). Television was in the process of ousting radio from its favoured position; radio of course was to remain popular, but competition from the flickering screen in the corner of the lounge had begun to take effect.

The Fifty Shilling Tailors was the place to go if you wanted to look reasonably smart on a limited budget. The sum of 50/- - two pounds fifty in today's currency (if not in value!) - would have paid for a smart and very serviceable suit of clothes - a must for any man being interviewed for a job, particularly as a salesman or a clerk. Some time in the 1950s the full name Fifty Shilling Tailors was abbreviated to 'FST', and the firm was later taken over by Colliers. A number of readers will no doubt remember their jolly little TV jingle informing viewers that John Colliers was 'the window to watch'!

A network of trolley bus wires lies far above the head of this cyclist in Westgate Street, and the fact that a bus is driving towards him emphasises the fact that two-way traffic was allowed back in January 1949. The shop on the corner of the Cornhill, which was at the time the rather smart Grimwade's outfitters, is today given over to cards of every description. On the right of the photograph, H Samuel's clock advises us that the time is 11.15, and judging by the number of people around, men as well as women, it was probably Saturday - everybody's shopping day. H Samuel's national slogan on the end of the clock reminds passers-by that they were the 'Empire's largest jeweller', a claim that brings to mind the historic days of the British Empire. Further

A glance at the 1950s

HOT OFF THE PRESS
The 1950s seemed to be the heyday of spies, and in 1951 the activities of Guy Burgess and Donald Maclean caused a sensation in the country. Both had occupied prominent positions in the Foreign Office, while Burgess had also been a member of MI-6.
Recruited by the Russians while at Cambridge University in the 1930s, the traitors provided the Soviets with a huge amount of valuable information. They disappeared in 1951, surfacing in Moscow five years later.

THE WORLD AT LARGE
Plans to develop the economies of member states into one common market came to fruition on 1st January 1958, when the EEC came into operation. The original members were France, Belgium, Luxembourg, The Netherlands, Italy, and West Germany. The Community became highly successful, achieving increased trade and prosperity across Western Europe while at the same time alleviating fear of war which lingered on after the end of World War II. Britain became a member in 1973.

ROYAL WATCH
King George VI's health had been causing problems since 1948, when he developed thrombosis. In 1951 the King - always a heavy smoker - became ill again, and was eventually found to be suffering from lung cancer. His left lung was removed in September of 1951. In January 1952 he waved Princess Elizabeth and Prince Philip off on their tour of Africa; they were never to see him again. The King died on 5th February 1952.

along on the right the Crown and Anchor was still serving Ipswich with their favourite brew. The pub dates back to the 1840s, though its ornate facade was built in 1897. Even earlier than that, two ancient inns, The Griffin and The Rampant Horse, stood on the site. Ipswich had no theatre at the time, and plays were staged in the yard behind The Griffin. The town's first theatre was founded by Henry Betts in 1736.

'Yes, we have some bananas....' In fact, this trader in Ipswich Market had nothing else but bananas on offer; he has obviously been able to secure a 'job lot' at a bargain price - and we are left wondering how much per pound he was inviting these punters to pay. Most of these shoppers seem to be enjoying themselves, however, judging by the wide smiles on many of the faces in the crowd. You could usually expect to pay a few coppers less for fruit and vegetables in the market than in the high street shops, and at closing time there were often real bargains to be snapped up if you happened to be in the

In the 1940s children had never seen a banana and had no idea that they had to peel off the skin

right place at the right time. The exact date of the photograph is not known to us, but it was certainly some time in the 1950s, a decade or so after the first bananas returned to our market stalls after the second world war. Back in 1946, a banana-starved populace welcomed the fruit back from the West Indies with open arms, while children born during the war had never seen a banana before, and had no idea that they had to peel off the skin before they could eat the fruit. The Home Secretary felt it necessary to put out a radio broadcast that gave children instructions how they should open and eat them.

Below: Christmas shopping; you either love it or hate it - but you still have to do it! Every shop you enter glitters with tinsel, Christmas trees and gifts, but it's after dark that Ipswich comes to brilliant life with hundreds of coloured lights that sparkle like gemstones in the darkness. This spectacular scene of Westgate Street at Christmas was caught on camera in 1964; people browse among the shops while traffic lines up on both sides of the street (now a pedestrian only area).

In today's commercially-minded society, Christmas trees, coloured lights and elaborate decorations find their way into the shops around the end of September, along with the endless gifts we are expected to spend thousands of pounds on. We would not wish for a return to the poverty that marked the early years of the 20th century, when Santa left few if any gifts in children's stockings - but oh, for those simple, non-materialistic Christmases!

Each year brings its own trend in gifts. The pressie

that Santa left under many a tree during the 1960s was a transistor radio - definitely the 'in' thing. The popularity of these novel miniature radios spread like the 'flu, quickly becoming all the rage, and no self-respecting teenager would be seen without his or her faithful 'tranny'! Pocket-sized transistor radios had been developed by the Japanese company Sony as early as 1952, though it took a few more years before they became widely available in Britain.

Bottom: Will he buy it - or won't he...? Weaver to Wearer's offer of an incredible 25 percent off raincoats was not to be sniffed at, and the attractive sale prices of the smart outfits in the window seem to have caught the eye of at least one potential customer. A group of ladies is approaching the photographer, and it is interesting to note how the fashion in shopping bags has changed over the years. It would take a sharp eye to spot the open wicker basket over one young woman's arm; large leather or plastic shopping bags are the choice of the others. Unhappily, pickpockets were largely responsible for the abandoning of those attractive baskets, and today we are more likely to carry the ever-present polythene carrier!

The names above the shop windows are not the only changes to have been made since this view of Carr Street was captured . The date was March 1966, and the street lamps like gigantic lollipops were typical of that decade. Since the time of the photograph, pedestrianisation has turned shopping into a far more comfortable experience, all the way from Carr Street and along Tavern Street to Westgate Street. In the distance we can see the Great White Horse - thankfully unchanged after more than 30 years. The Eastgate Shopping Centre today adds its own flavour to Carr Street.

Above: Which clock is telling the right time? This photograph reveals an interesting situation: the clock on Milletts' corner informs us that it is four-thirty, while the neighbouring clock mounted on the wall of the jewellers further along Tavern Street begs to differ, arguing that the time is two-twenty-five. Whatever the time, though, the shoppers are out in full force, taking advantage of the sunny September day. Back in 1967 - the year of the photograph - they would have had to dodge the traffic in Tavern Street; today's paved areas and pedestrian precincts have brought a wonderfully relaxed atmosphere to shopping in the town centre. The attractive Georgian facade of the Great White Horse on the right is just that - a facade. Behind it lies a little piece of Ipswich history, the original wall of the timber framed building that dates back to the 1700s. If plaques were mounted in the hotel's bedrooms to mark the resting-places of the famous they would not read 'Queen Elizabeth slept here'. They would, however, include King George II, King Louis XVIII of France, Lord Nelson and Charles Dickens. We cannot say how much Dickens might have paid for bed and breakfast at the Great White Horse, but back in 1967, B&B would have set you back between 45/- and 65/- (£2.25 to £3.25). A good dinner could be had for 10/6d (around 53p).

Right: Where did they all go to? Police officers on point duty, that is. There was a time when every major junction in every major town had its traffic 'bobby'; remember those black and white zebra-striped boxes they used to use? The boxes made them highly visible and gave them the elevation and air of authority they needed. Point duty must have demanded a high concentration of manpower, however, and it was no doubt argued that instead of directing the town's traffic the police force would be better employed in concentrating their efforts on the fight against crime. So a few at a time they departed, leaving the motorist with a legacy of traffic lights to contend with at each junction. Traffic lights, while no doubt keeping the traffic flowing smoothly through the town centre (in theory at least), somehow lack the personal touch provided by the good old British bobby.

The services of these two guardians of law and order appear to have been largely unneeded, as we see no sign of traffic on Hyde Park Corner or St Matthews Street. The Rainbow pub, which stood to the left of the photograph, was demolished in the 1960s and St Matthews Street became the wide dual carriageway we know today. The photograph was taken in January 1956; we can assume by the warm coats and boots of these passers-by that the weather was chilly.

At work

Below: 'No hat, no boots, no job...?' The flat caps worn by these steeplejacks working high above the ground were the hardest hats on site when the incinerator chimney at the Anglesea Road hospital was demolished in September 1963. And although they might have been wearing boots, their protective goggles are pushed up on top of their heads, risking the danger of chips of concrete from their pneumatic drills flying into their eyes. The slogan that reflects today's emphasis on workers' safety had no meaning thirty-odd years ago, when employees still undertook many dangerous jobs every day without gauntlets, safety glasses, hard hats or protective clothing of any kind, reflecting very little on the risk factor. In fact, in some occupations it was regarded as being somewhat less than macho to wear protective clothing!

The original hospital was built on the higher ground of Anglesea Road in 1836. Over the years a children's wing and other departments were added to the Victorian building, and by 1909 the hospital had the capacity to take 2,000 in-patients and an incredible 10,000 out-patients every year. Eventually Ipswich was provided with a new hospital in Heath Road, and much of the former facility was demolished. Today the only part remaining is the original Victorian structure, which lives on as Anglesea Heights, a residential nursing home.

The men in this photograph might be described as a couple of thorns in a whole bouquet of roses! The bulk of Philips and Piper's workforce was obviously female, and without a doubt the few males dotted around the factory would have come in for a lot of teasing and leg-pulling during the working day. Every machine was buzzing on the day the sewing room was caught on camera in September 1963, and these girls were had at work producing the high class riding gear and gentlemen's formal evening wear for which the company was renowned. Philips and Piper provided employment in the town until fairly recently - it only closed down in 1982. It was during the second world war that many more women went out to work, some of them for the first time, turning generations of tradition upside down. After the war many of them didn't want to give up their jobs and go back to their old lives; they had become used to the degree of independence that a weekly wage gave them. Suddenly they could afford to buy clothes and makeup and treats for the children!

When Philips and Piper closed its doors the building was converted to use as flats, which today are very pleasant and enjoy good security, which has unfortunately not always been the case for Pipers Court.

A glance at the 1950s

MELODY MAKERS
Few teenage girls could resist the blatant sex-appeal of 'Elvis the Pelvis', though their parents were scandalised at the moody Presley's provocatively gyrating hips. The singer took America and Britain by storm with such hits as 'Jailhouse Rock', 'All Shook Up' and 'Blue Suede Shoes'. The rhythms of Bill Haley and his Comets, Buddy Holly, Chuck Berry, and Roy Orbison (who had a phenomenal three-octave voice) turned the 1950s into the Rock 'n' Roll years.

INVENTION AND TECHNOLOGY
Until the late 1950s you did not carry radios around with you. Radios were listened to at home, plugged into a mains socket in every average sitting room. Japan was in the forefront of electronic developments even then, and in 1957 the Japanese company Sony introduced the world's very first all-transistor radio - an item of new technology that was small enough to fit into your pocket. The major consumer product caught on fast - particularly with teenage listeners.

SCIENCE AND DISCOVERY
DNA (deoxyribonucleic acid) was first defined as long ago as 1953, and the effects have been far-reaching. The key discovery was developed over the following years and today DNA finger-printing has become an accepted part of life. Genetic diseases such as hemophilia and cystic fibrosis have been identified. Criminals are continually detected and brought to justice. Biological drugs have been developed. More controversially, drought and disease-resistant plants have been engineered - and Dolly the sheep has been produced.

It was 1930 when this cheerful road gang working in Lower Brook Street snatched a few minutes to stop working and pose for the camera. Three little schoolgirls in wide-brimmed hats add their own brand of charm to the scene. No matter what kind of work is in progress, gangs of men working have always attracted passers-by to watch them; dig a hole, and people gather to gaze into it! Perhaps these girls had been watching the progress of the work when the photographer set up his camera -

stayed to be included in the resulting photograph? Photography was of course well advanced by the 1930s, though few ordinary families had a camera of their own. Well into the 1940s 'having your photograph taken' remained a rather special occasion, and the presence of a man with a camera still had novelty value. And why was the photograph taken, we wonder? Was it to mark a particular occasion, or did the foreman one day suddenly say, 'I know - let's have our picture taken'? It's impossible to know, but interesting to speculate....

The man on the left is sitting on blocks of tar, piled up ready to go into the tar boiler. The piece of machinery in the background is intriguing. It has a drive belt, and it worked, of course, by steam. Could this perhaps have been a stone crusher?

Above: The gentle curve that was to become the Princes Street round-about can already be seen taking shape here, supported by hoardings, as the redevelopment of the town centre took Ipswich swinging into the 1960s. The build-up of traffic had caused its own problems over the years, and ambitious plans to keep vehicles moving smoothly through the town via an improved traffic system with one-way streets, wide dual carriageways, pedestrian only areas and of course the inevitable traffic lights had been created a few years earlier. The plans involved a massive clearance of shops and residential areas and by the mid 1960s the bulldozers, compressors, cranes and scaffolders moved in along with gangs of men with shovels, and very shortly vast areas of land had been reduced to heaps of rubble. From it rose the Greyfriars block - the vantage point from which this view was captured. Today, the roundabout that eventually emerged from this construction site occupies the foreground of this view. Much of the housing on the left was cleared to make way for a new road to link St Matthews Street with Civic Drive. The flat roof of the Mann Egerton building can be seen on the left of the photograph.

Right: Bricks and rubble are all that remain of what was once a close-knit community, and William Street, Fitzroy Street, Peel Street, Beck Street, Chenery Street and Charles Street have disappeared under the onslaught of the bulldozer. The years of the mid 1960s were years of radical change that saw the redevelopment of areas that had been familiar in the town for generations. The streets where people had grown up, the pubs where they had for many years spent their Saturday evenings, the services they relied on and the corner shops where they felt comfortable and whose proprietors they knew and exchanged gossip with, all were to be swept away and their inhabitants dispersed to other, more unfamiliar, parts of Ipswich. Many would have been dreading the day when they had to move out of their old homes. On the other hand there would have been those, partic-ularly perhaps the younger couples with a growing family, who would have been eagerly looking forward to the move.

Even in the 1960s not a few families were still living in cramped condi-tions, perhaps with few modern conveniences. We have to hope that those who were rehoused were happy in their new homes, and that their sense of community would before long be re-established in a different area of the town.

The Group that keeps expanding by contracting

The early 1950s was a period of significant urban development, creating plenty of work for civil engineering contractors and providing opportunities for good, new firms. On 30 June 1952 one such company was founded. Mr Frank Jackson was appointed Director, his wife, Mrs Janet Jackson was appointed Secretary, and the company was registered as Roadworks (1952) Limited. Within a year Roadworks had established itself at 55/61 Commercial Road, Ipswich. With a capital of £1,000 and overdraft facilities of up to £2,000, Frank fitted out the premises and purchased the necessary plant, including some very fine steamrollers, all smartly painted with the Roadworks (1952) Limited logo.

Investment in machinery and equipment is a major but necessary expense for any construction company, and from the outset Frank Jackson made a virtue of necessity. Not only did he make sure he had the necessary equipment for the job, acquiring at an early stage machines such as pavers for use in surfacing work, but he also had the foresight to realise that specialised equipment was a good investment in its own right. This was to pay dividends in subsequent years.

Roadworks' workforce - initially eight workmen, supervised by Frank Jackson - had an excellent team spirit, and during the first decade they worked on projects at Orford, Felixstowe, and Levington Research Station; they also re-surfaced the drive leading to Grundisburgh House, built a 4.5 mile section of the Woodbridge By-pass, and undertook road and infrastructure works at the Chelsworth Avenue housing site in Ipswich. Since projects varied so much in size, Frank soon set up a special department to concentrate on small but important works such as house, estate and farm driveways. No matter how large or small the job, the company aimed to give customers good quality and timely completion, and by the end of the 50s Roadworks Limited was well-known and respected throughout East Anglia.

During the 60s the company's work continued to expand, with a corresponding diversification in corporate structure. Two core divisions were set up; highways projects were carried out by Roadworks and building work by F J Construction. Subsidiaries were set up to provide services to civil engineering and other industries; Anglia Plant Limited hired out plant and equipment, and transport services were

Top left: *Company founder Mr Frank Jackson.* **Above right:** *The Commercial Road premises in the early 1950s.* **Right:** *A very early steam powered road roller.*

provided by Biscoe Transport in Britannia Road. All the subsidiaries were part of the Jackson Group, with its headquarters in a new office block at Dobbs Lane, Kesgrave - built, of course, by F J Construction.

Around this time Roadworks, meanwhile, was involved in major schemes at Felixstowe and Ipswich Docks, and at the A45/A14 junction at Caxton Gibbett. By this time there were also Roadworks depots at School Lane, Norwich, another in Cambridge and a third in Chelmsford. Contracts were being undertaken over a wide geographical area, and the workforce now numbered well into the hundreds; but the team spirit was maintained, and Frank Jackson took care not to lose touch with happenings within the Company. A company newsletter was instituted, and a most important meeting was held in November 1968, where the matter for discussion was the setting up of a Football Club; a Committee was duly appointed, comprising representatives from Blacktop Supplies, F J Construction, Anglia Plant, Biscoe Transport and Roadworks, and presided over by Frank Jackson himself.

The 1970s brought many large contracts for F J Construction, among them the building of a large Solar foodstore for the Ipswich Co-operative Society. This £714,000 Supermarket was the first of its kind in Ipswich and was completed in 1977. A motel and high security park complex at Felixstowe for Securicor and new premises for Days Garage at Lowestoft, comprising showrooms, workshops, stores and offices were other

significant projects. Meanwhile Roadworks, benefiting from a new and much faster asphalt plant, which was commissioned in 1971, was busy with the £1m Balkerne Hill section of the Colchester Inner Relief Road, a major scheme incorporating a new interchange and footbridge; it was completed on schedule and local dignitaries at the opening ceremony, performed in April 1977, included the Lord Lieutenant of Essex Sir John Ruggles-Brize, Mayor Mrs Joyce Brooks, and Mr Frank Jackson. In 1976 in Ipswich work was carried out to re-develop the Electric House car park into a bus terminal, for the Ipswich Borough Buses.

Also in 1976 Jackson Group acquired the small Woodbridge building company F Ingram Smith and was soon able to restore it to profitability. This traditional firm had a reputation for employing highly skilled craftsmen, and as part of the Jackson Group went on to specialise in restoration work on churches, period houses and heritage buildings of many kinds, consistently winning awards for the quality of craftsmanship. Meanwhile the Group's other subsidiaries continued to return good profits. Frank Jackson had been quick to recognise that compressed air equipment could play an important role in civil engineering; Anglia Plant opened a workshop in Witham, and at the beginning of the 70s, as compressed air equipment grew increasingly sophis-

Top: Roadbuilding in Felixstowe, 1956.
Below: Working on Foxhall Stadium, 1966/67.

Left: Chelsworth Avenue in the mid 1950s.
Below: Woodbridge By-Pass pictured shortly after its completion.

beached, while the other was welded to the bow section to maintain buoyancy.

The Jackson Group celebrated its Silver Jubilee in 1977 by announcing its plans to become a public company, anticipating that this status would bring the Group more prestige and thus give it more scope to build on the tremendous success it had achieved during its first 25 years. Record profits and

ticated and was exploited in a variety of applications, Anglia Pneumatics was set up in Luton to sell and service compressors of all sizes. In 1978 Anglia Plant was able to play a vital part in helping to avert catastrophe in the North Sea when the tanker Eleni V ran aground; it supplied two compressors, one which helped raise the hull and keep it afloat until it could be

turnover had been achieved for successive years between 1971 and 1976, and 1977 was no exception, bringing a turnover of £9,312,498 and a net profit of £504,374. The Group was to operate successfully as a public company for ten years before applying to be listed on The Stock Exchange, and since 1987 has gone on to even greater achievements.

A steady flow of major by-pass contracts continued to come the Company's way following its conversion to a public company in 1977. Construction began on both the Beccles by-pass and the March by-pass in 1980. The £5.5m by-pass near Kings Lynn was completed in 1982 and the £3.75m Ampthill by-pass in Bedfordshire was completed in November 1983. In 1985 bypasses under construction included Sudbury in Suffolk, Great Hockham, and Ely and Littleport. The £5.6m Martlesham by-pass was begun in July 1986, and in 1989 work started on the £4.4m Long Melford by-pass and the £7.5m Shefford by-pass. Meanwhile, more locally, the Ipswich by-pass Eastern section had been completed well ahead of time and declared open by Mrs Lynda Chalker, Minister of Transport, on 5 June 1984. This scheme, covering the 4.5 km between the Gloster Road roundabout at Martlesham Heath and the A45 interchange at Seven Hills, and involving such varied civil engineering challenges as the construction of a roundabout at Foxhall Road, an overbridge at Bucklesham Road, a culvert where Mill River crosses under the by-pass and a stable embankment to carry the road over the river valley, had cost in excess of £3m.

Towards the end of the 1970's the Group had reviewed its position and decided to concentrate on extending

Roadworks' civil engineering capabilities beyond traditional highways construction. Successful bids for railway work, sea defences, water and sewage systems, environmental improvements and industrial construction followed, and memorable projects in the 1980s included environmental work at Beckton Lake and the construction of the British Rail line into Stansted Airport. At Felixstowe the company built the rail link to the docks - the first new British Rail track in the region since 1906 - and other coastal improvements included the sea wall below Latimer House, and The Dip. F J Construction's achievements during the decade included the £3.2m Custom House for Property Services Agency at Felixstowe and the £5m Ipswich Crown pools complex which won the Suffolk Association of Architects' award for general craftsmanship. On a smaller scale, subsidiary Ingram Smith continued to live up to its reputation for quality work, undertaking the redevelopment of a number of period properties in the centre of Woodbridge to provide

Top: *Early road surfacing equipment, a Weavers lorry and the Company's very first paver.* ***Above:*** *Her Majesty Queen Elizabeth the Queen Mother opens the Histon By-Pass, November 7th 1963. Mr Frank Jackson is on the right of the picture.*

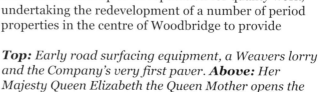

***Left:** Making the move to bigger offices in 1966. **Bottom:** The original Solar Foodstore after its opening in 1978.*

sales. The 12-storey St Clare House, in the centre of Ipswich, was bought by the Group in 1987, completely refurbished by F J Construction and leased to Property Services Agency, before being sold for some £5.55m in May 1992; in spite of the recession this still represented an overall profit in excess of £1m.

The formation of the Property Division also had an impact on the work of F J Construction, as the Group's own building projects began to feature heavily in its workload. Another development in the trade

superior private residences, and winning awards for work carried out at Suffolk's historic County Hall and for the new Headmaster's House at Woodbridge School.

The 1980s also brought redefinition of the roles of the Group's smaller subsidiaries. Pneumatic equipment continued to be a growth area, and the early 80s saw the acquisition of ATC Pneumatics, which later merged with Anglia Pneumatics to become Anglair Limited. Another subsidiary, Factair, was set up to design and produce its own equipment, and almost immediately this led to the Group undertaking a contract to install a complex breathing-air supply within the British Steel gas holders at the Port Talbot steelworks. Significant orders for equipment followed, such as the £500,000 contract to supply 400 special compressors for a government department. The Group then moved into a completely new sphere by establishing an active interest in property development and management through the formation of a Property Division, to be known as Jackson Projects Limited. Having entered property management in the early 80s, the company had by the end of the decade launched office, retail, industrial, housing and sheltered home developments. Although the fall in property prices in the early 90s hit the Property Division, the Group's considerable investment in property proved invaluable during the recession, when it was able to release funds through property

was the introduction and growing popularity of Design & Build as an extremely cost and time-efficient method of construction; from 1987 onwards this type of project provided F J Construction with an increasing proportion of its turnover; in 1992, when the recession was causing problems in the building industry, the company was able to capitalise on its Design & Build expertise, carrying out projects outside its normal region and as far afield as Edinburgh and Southampton, which proved useful in offsetting the declining demand elsewhere.

Roadworks managed to weather the depression thanks to substantial projects such as the £8.4m Castor/Ailsworth by-pass which was completed in 1992, the £8.4m project to reconstruct a section of the A13 as dual carriageway near Southend, and in 1993 a £5m improvement scheme was begun on the A11, which led to a £24m adjoining dual carriageway scheme in 1994/95.

Anglia Plant and Anglair began to show reduced profits during the difficult trading conditions of the early 1990s, but this was remedied by reorganisation and investment in computers and other facilities which improved the level of customer service, increased their competitiveness and within a short time restored and enhanced profitability.

Nineteen ninety-six brought many changes to the Group, although in fact many of these simply formalised the shifts in emphasis which had come about over a number of years. Roadworks was renamed Jackson Civil Engineering, a move which both reflected the fact that its capabilities now extended far beyond highway construction, and at the same time established corporate identity; this was reinforced by the renaming of FJ Construction as Jackson Building, the transport division, Biscoe, as Jackson Haulage and the site plant division as Jackson Plant. It was in this year, too, that Frank Jackson retired after heading the company for over 40 years. He was succeeded briefly by Peter Green and Dr Robin Turrell before David Jackson, the current Chairman, took over in 1998.

Recent years have confirmed the wisdom of the company's policy of widening the skills base of the Civil Engineering division. Revised national policy on roads has led to decreased expenditure on new road construction, and railway engineering has become an important facet of Jackson Civil Engineering's work, with a rail division being launched in 1998 called Jackson Rail. Factair has complemented this involvement with rail by developing projects with rail-related applications. The 'Extended Arm' Contract for Railtrack PLC has involved the company in a substantial maintenance and renewal programme for

the South Anglia area over a four-year period, while the company has also completed contracts for Railtrack Southern and London Underground. Other civil engineering projects include Welmore Sluice in the Fens for the Environment Agency; access roads and infrastructure for the Bluewater Shopping Centre in Kent and major works for the Ports of Tilbury, Felixstowe and Harwich. Jackson Building's recent major projects include a new maltings for Pauls Malt Limited at Bury St Edmunds and a £10m distribution warehouse in Coventry. Also offices and warehouse facilities have been built for John Menzies at Ransomes Europark in Ipswich and Edward le Bas at Claydon. Ingram Smith was privileged to carry out the renovation of a Napoleonic fort at Felixstowe in 1997/8 for English Heritage. The Group's newest acquisition Scofield and Lait Roofing Limited has given the company in-house specialised building services to complement its general building skills.

The Group is firmly committed to quality and training. Anglair holds accreditation to ISO 9002, and the quality management of Jackson Civil Engineering, Jackson Building, Ingram Smith and Factair has been approved to BS EN ISO 9001. For many years the Group has promoted site safety, liaising with local schools and councils, and in 1996 Jackson Civil Engineering received Anglian Water's Golden Helmet Award for safest construction site.

The evolution of the Group continued in January 1999 with its merger with a Yorkshire-based construction group, Peterhouse Group Plc. The greatly increased size of the Group will enable it to tender for larger jobs, in a wider geographical area, although Jackson Group's commitment to its roots in East Anglia will not change.

The Jackson Group can look back at almost half a century's success, based on sound engineering skills deployed by competent and far-sighted management; and with its Golden Jubilee now in sight it can rest assured that those same qualities will assure its success for at least as far into the future.

Top left: *In 1976, Roadworks converted the Electric House car park in Ipswich to a bus terminal.*
Top right: *Shows construction work on St Clare House, with Ipswich Town Football Club in the background.*

The family firm where innovation, consistency and good value are just part of the furniture

At present-day property prices, London's Chelsea is not the most obvious choice of location for a cabinet-maker's workshop. That, however, is where Mr William Alston laid the foundation for the Alston family business when he began repairing and restoring furniture for south-west Londoners, back in 1760. By 1840 the family had begun manufacturing fine, hand-crafted furniture; and by that time, too, it had moved to East Anglia.

The family business became established in Sudbury, Suffolk, where until 1920 all its furniture was still hand-made and the only machine to be found in its workshops was a lathe. Having been handed down through successive generations, the business was by this time in the hands of Percy Alston, grandson of the founder and an eminent local figure, being twice elected Mayor. It was his son Leslie who took the step of introducing machines into the workshop. This decision was taken in the wake of the first world war, which had left many people in financial difficulties, and greatly reduced the market for the bespoke, high-class, individual pieces of furniture which the firm had up to now specialised in. Leslie, who had served a six-year apprenticeship in the East End of London where he had gained a first-hand acquaintance with the modern manufacturing methods of the day, wholeheartedly supported the use of machinery as a means of bringing the cost of good quality furniture down to an affordable level.

By 1937 Alstons, now being run by Leslie Alston, had moved into the mid-priced sector of the market and was producing some 60 pieces of good-value furniture a week at a new, larger factory, fitted out with all the latest machinery, in nearby Long Melford. When war came the Government Utility Scheme was launched, under which furniture production was to be limited to basic items of dining room and bedroom furniture made to designs specified by the government; because Alstons was already mechanised and its workforce was fully experienced on the machines, it was quickly able to adapt to the manufacture of utility furniture, and was one of the first 40 or 50 firms to begin production. Coffins were also manufactured in quantity. However, with production in full swing the factory itself became a casualty of enemy action; on the night of October 12th, 1942 fire consumed practically the whole factory area, with only the showroom, offices and veneering section escaping destruction. Leslie Alston immediately began to search for new premises, and was soon able to make arrangements to share the premises of Messrs Wrinch, a firm which was engaged on war work and the manufacture of school furniture in a factory on Nacton Road, Ipswich.

The arrangement worked surprisingly well, and the two firms continued to operate from the same premises for some seven years, but nonetheless Alstons was naturally keen to acquire premises of its own again as soon as possible. For several years after the war it remained notoriously difficult to get planning permission to build new factories, and obtaining permits for steel and

Below: *The factory prior to opening in 1949.*

building materials was all but impossible. However, Mr Alston was determined to find a way. He was fortunate in that land was available adjacent to the Nacton Road site, and this he managed to purchase. The next problem was to get a building erected on it. His building licence stated that he must provide his own materials and labour, and he hit upon the perfect source - the many airfields in the surrounding area each housed a number of disused Romney huts as well as piles of redundant war material. He was able to acquire as many Romney huts as he needed, and all that remained was to dismantle them, move them to Nacton Road and reassemble them to make a factory. Leslie Alston worked out an ingenious plan, and by 1949 Alstons had their factory; nicknamed 'The Tunnel', it consisted of lots of Romney huts joined end-to-end, to form a

structure a third of a mile long and 40 feet wide. Having a long thin building brought its own advantages: during manufacture, an item simply progressed from one end to the other, undergoing its various production processes along the way, so that in theory this eliminated all the moving backwards and forwards between one department and another that can occur in a more conventionally-shaped factory.

Shortly after the completion of the 'Tunnel' factory, Leslie was joined by his elder son John. The company was able to diversify its range of products; in 1951 the decision was made to enter the upholstery field,

Above: *The mill in the new factory shortly after opening in 1949.*

although initially only on a modest scale, and Colchester became the centre of these activities. Overall the business resumed the expansion that had been planned before the war, and by 1956 around 250 people were employed at the factory. In the early 60s Leslie's younger son Alan joined the team. The upholstery side of the business had proved a success and had grown steadily, with over 600 pieces being made each week by the end of 1963; and it was upholstery which gave the company its first major breakthrough into the export market, with Holland and Belgium providing a significant outlet for upholstery items between 1962 and 1973. During 1963 Alan Alston supervised the building of a brand new, purpose-built upholstery factory which began production in January 1964. Since that time production methods have advanced considerably, and today improved models are produced at the rate of 1450 pieces a week.

Meanwhile the Romney huts had continued to serve their purpose in Ipswich and were very good at keeping the rain out, but by the end of the 60s the company felt that it was time to think about rebuilding the factory. Architect John Adams drew up plans, and construction work began in 1971. The work was originally scheduled to be carried out over ten years, in such a way that it would not be necessary to halt production; the new factory was to be erected directly over the existing works, which would then be demolished as construction progressed. The new office block was the last

part to be built. In the event work progressed more swiftly than had been anticipated. The office block was completed by the end of June, 1976; this signified the completion of the entire rebuilding project, and it had all been accomplished without holding up production even for an hour. Sadly, Leslie Alston did not live to see the new factory in full production; he died in March 1976, leaving his two sons to carry on in his footsteps until June 1990 when sadly his elder son John died.

Alan Alston took over the complete reins of the group in May 1979 and in August 1995 handed over the daily running of the business to his two sons John and David

Below (Both pictures): *. Views of the finishing shops.*

Alston. John takes special responsibility for cabinet bedroom furniture and David is in charge of upholstery, which has grown into a very important side of Alston's activities. The company has always avoided being too bureaucratic in its approach, finding that by keeping a simple structure it is able to make decisions quickly and act on them promptly. The strong family involvement which has always been a major feature of the company has formed the basis of the friendly relationships which have grown up with both customers and suppliers. Alstons has been using many of its suppliers for up to 30 years or more, and this ensures that the buying process runs smoothly as suppliers are accustomed to complying with the company's quality requirements and adhering to its policy of sourcing all components and raw materials from within the European Community. Similarly, retailers are kept abreast of all the company's developments. They are invited to previews of new ranges in the specially built showrooms at the factory site, and their comments are welcomed; they are also encouraged to visit the factories and watch the production processes, and again are invited to discuss future design projects. The company is also a prominent exhibitor at major furniture exhibitions, where both new and existing customers can view their products.

The company's policy - to make good, well-designed furniture which the public can afford - began under Leslie Alston and has continued to this day; and another of Leslie Alston's principles which has remained crucial to the firm's development is that of equipping the factory with the best machines for the job. Leslie Alston developed one of the first all-electric machine shops for producing furniture, and this policy of innovation has continued, ensuring that today's methods of production are as fully automated as technology and practicality allow. As soon as the technology to mechanise a process becomes available, the company makes the investment. At the same time a programme of continual replacement of machinery is operated, which ensures that no machine is more than seven years old; this, the company believes, is the best way to achieve consistency in production and improvement of product. In line with its policy of investing in the most up-to-date production techniques, Alstons installed its first computer in the early 1960s. The firm has now progressed to a computer system which operates on

Above (both pictures): A fire in April 1952 prompted the company to issue this leaflet, asking for forbearance during the reconstruction.

twin mini-computers linked to over 100 terminals and PCs and which is totally integrated across every aspect of the business. Payroll, accounts, purchases, sales, product design, production and work-in-progress data are all instantly accessible; a barcode system allows the production flowline to be monitored at every stage, from purchase of raw materials right through to despatch on the firm's own delivery vehicles, and there is on-line access to sales order processing, which means that the company can respond immediately to customers enquiries on the progress of orders and any other query which may arise. With production at the Ipswich factory now running at up to 10,000 units a week, and a total workforce of 430, the computer system is vital in maintaining quality of product and quality of service. In this sphere as in every other the company is constantly on the look-out for ways of lowering the risk of error or misunderstanding and increasing efficiency. To this end manual input is kept to a minimum, while another relatively recent innovation has been the introduction of electronic data interchange (EDI) which allows a number of customers to place orders on-line.

The company is also firmly committed to providing all its services in-house rather than using sub-contractors, as it is convinced that in this way it can deliver a better-controlled, better-quality service to the customer. This applies particularly to its despatch and distribution services. Alstons operates its own fleet of delivery vehicles; its smart Volvos trucks, resplendent in their green livery with the company's red and yellow logo with black and white lettering, are a familiar sight on the county's roads and beyond.

Ipswich, of course, is fortunate in being particularly well-placed on both the national trunk road network and the overseas traffic routes, so that in fact Alston's is able to deliver to mainland Europe are as quickly and easily as within the UK.

Top: *The factory extension being built during the 1950s.*
Above left: *John Alston, MD Cabinets.*
Above right: *David Alston, MD Upholstery.*
Right: *Alston maintains a close relationship with retailers.*

Another area which has been greatly changed by technology is that of furniture design, which is now in the hands of small design teams who use the latest computer-aided design techniques to create the shapes of the future. From there, each stage of the production process is a quality centre with a skilled workforce using the latest machinery and techniques, and monitoring the quality of their output by means of 'quality circles' within the production team.

For a family firm to continue in same trade for 240 year is a remarkable achievement. Alstons has stood the test of time, and because teamwork and innovation are both well-established company tradition its products and services are guaranteed to please its customers. Today, with everything at Alston's geared towards quality and consistency, the company's overriding commitment is to putting the customer first and making sure that every customer gets real value, every time.

Top: Part of Alston's fleet of delivery vehicles.
Left: Automated assembly of furniture. *Below:* Mr Alan Alston, Chairman of the company.

The international transport company which enjoys success all along the road

Ipswich, with its connections, its excellent transport links and its growth in size and prosperity which began in the mid-19th century, has attracted many a business to make its home here. The presence of Ferrymasters - now a fully-owned subsidiary of P&O Trans European - in Ipswich can be traced back to the work of Lancashire businessman and haulier Mr Ted Percival and his successors. In 1953 Ted Percival started a haulage business in Preston, Lancashire. Initially, he specialised in carrying freight from mainland UK to Belfast, and so with impeccable logic he named his venture Northern Ireland Transport Services (NITS). Before long, however, the business had diversified into carrying from the UK to destinations in mainland Europe. An association with European Ferries in Felixstowe was formed, and East Anglia has remained an important base for the company ever since; it came to Ipswich in 1976 as a result of a growing collaboration with North Sea Ferries, and this developed into a full-scale joint venture in the mid 1980s.

During its early years of operations, the company had used the roll-on, roll-off (ro-ro) method of operation for its cargo freight services, which involved simply driving the vehicle onto a ferry at the departure point, and driving off the other side when the ferry arrived at its destination. However, the Suez crisis, which flared up in the mid-50s and rumbled on for a decade or so, put an end to this practice because the Government promptly comandeered all the ro-ro ferries. As a result all cargo operators were compelled to change their practices, and Ted Percival, along with many others, had to switch to the lift-on, lift-off system.

Top right: *A 10ft Lancashire Flat waiting to load automotive spares.* **Left:** *Northern Ireland Transport Services trucks awaiting deliveries in Eire.*

Meanwhile the company's successful expansion into UK-Europe traffic had brought with it one slight problem: it meant that the company's original name of Northern Ireland Transport Services was no longer an accurate description of its activities. A new name was needed which would reflect the growing importance of the international aspect of the company's business. In true democratic style, the company decided to hold a competition among its staff, and everybody was invited to think of a new name. Many good suggestions were received, but the competition was won by the inspired employee who thought up the name Ferrymasters. From then on clients' warehouse and despatch staff soon got used to looking out for the arrival of the distinctive and highly visible yellow trailers, smartly emblazoned with the name of Ferrymasters in black lettering.

Ted Percival remained at the head of Northern Ireland Transport Services, alias Ferrymasters, until 1964 when he left to pursue other interests; he subsequently rejoined the company, however, becoming Managing Director and Chairman and continuing to give valuable service to the firm for a

Top right: *A 20ft Flat laden with machinery awaiting export.*
Right: *The management team circa 1969.* **Below:** *Machinery awaiting shipment.*

total of almost twenty years. As the company grew and as its reputation became established in the transport industry, Ted Percival was fortunate in being able to attract the services of a number of experienced senior management personnel from British Road Services (BRS), including Ted Hains and Ron Green who became Operations Directors.

In 1967 the Head Office of the growing company was set up in Altrincham, Cheshire. It was during the mid 1970s that Ted Percival decided it was time for him to hand over the running of the thriving operation which he had been instrumental in establishing, and Geoff Whitehead, who had been involved from the outset, took over. Geoff continued to build up the business. Over the years many people have played their part in the firm's continued success; Ted Percival of course heads the list, and tribute must also be paid to Geoff Whitehead and the managing directors who succeeded him: Mr Van Shindel, Mr Brian Rosier, the late Mr Jim Brook, Mr Derek Munt and Mr John Bradshaw who for many

years ensured the smooth running of operations in Altrincham.

The company's success continued when its operations came under the P&O Ferrymasters banner, and it became universally recognised as an established market leader in the provision of extensive, integrated European transport services. The name P&O will of course be familiar to many people, for many different reasons. Some associate them with holidays; others might remember that in 1982 MV Elk, one of P&O's roll-on roll-off vessels, was commandeered for service in the Falklands as a supplies and ammunition carrier. However, while virtually everybody in Ipswich knows the name P&O and the blue, white, red and yellow flag which is its logo, probably not everybody

Top: An early left hand drive Scania en-route to a German delivery. **Above:** *The certificate presented to P&O following the successful return of their ship "Elk" after her time as a supplies and ammunition carrier during the Falklands War in 1982.*

knows that the company's full name is in fact 'The Peninsular and Oriental Steam Navigation Company'; or that the flag takes its blue and white colours from the Portuguese Royal House and its red and yellow colours from the Spanish Royal House. This represents the roots of the company on the Iberian peninsula. In 1837, when it first began operating, its key activity consisted of delivering the post from Great Britain to Portugal and Spain. Three years later it received the order for the handling of the monthly post shipments to Alexandria, in Egypt; this extension to its activities supplied the 'Oriental' to its name and also laid the financial foundation for subsequent growth. By 1843 its service had extended to India, by 1845 to China and by 1852 to Australia, and from then it continued to expand its steamboat services for post and passenger to become a substantial company in England. Its domination of the world shipping industry came about through the purchase of other shipping companies in the first part of the 20th century.

Today P&O Ferrymasters' main markets lie in Benelux, Germany and Scandinavia, with clients including Shell, ICI, Compaq, Mercedes Benz, Kodak and Ford. With a policy of continued investment in both the personal development of its employees and the resources at their disposal, a quality system registered to BS EN ISO 9002, and a fundamental commitment to adopting and observing the customer's definition of service, P&O Ferrymasters today continues its tradition of fulfilling and exceeding customer expectation, and thus maintain its market leading position.

Top: Norsky loading at Ipswich.
Below: An early arrival in Holland.

A tradition of service to the local community

Records show that the Jackaman family was already established in the legal profession in Ipswich at the end of the 18th Century. By 1799 at the age of 26 Simon Jackaman, a descendant of Simon Jackaman florist and gardener, who had died in 1784, was in practice as the first lawyer in the family and the holder of a number of civic offices. He was elected a common Councillor in 1800, in 1803 he became one of the town's two bailiffs or governors, and he was subsequently Town Clerk, Treasurer to the Association for the Prosecution of Felons, and Clerk to the Port Commissioners. He was also a church warden at St. Nicholas Church.

His apprenticeship as a solicitor had been served with William Bately, and in 1799 he married Sarah Bately his former boss's daughter. It is thought the family occupied substantial land and property adjacent to the River Gipping south of where the Greyfriars development now stands, perhaps on the site of Jewson's warehouse. Simon and Sarah's son, Simon Batley Jackaman, was born in 1801 and he, like his father, decided to pursue a career in the law. At the age of 2 1 Simon Batley Jackaman became an attorney at law and coroner for Ipswich. Like his father, he carried out all his duties with great assiduity, but paid particular attention (if we choose to believe the local gossip of the day) to his duties as coroner - it is said that he used to send his clerk down to the port to make sure that any corpses which happened to be floating in the dock were landed ashore within his jurisdiction (which, incidentally, ensured that he secured a fee).

Between 1834 and 1836 Simon Batley Jackaman moved the practice to offices in Silent Street, which he is believed to have inherited from his grandfather William Bately. He was in practice for a total of 50 years, during which time he was held in the highest esteem by the local people. He retired in 1873 and died two years later. At his funeral, he was accorded last respects "as a lawyer ... for soundness of judgement combined with great acuteness" as "an upright man... a kindly and chivalrous man" and as "a Conservative of the best type" who fought his political battles hard but fairly and honourably. The following year a memorial window was erected in St. Nicholas Church in his memory.

Simon Batley Jackaman was succeeded by his sons Henry Mason Jackaman and William Batley Jackaman. Both had been admitted as attorneys at law, and records of the firm as Messrs. Jackaman & Sons indicate that the brothers had practised in partnership with their father for a time, but the family practice then seems to have passed to H. M. Jackaman. He took into partnership another Ipswich solicitor, Henry William Miller, who paid a premium of £1,200 for a 12 year partnership agreement, subsequently renewed for life. From about 1895 until H. W. Miller's retirement in 1916 the firm was known as Jackaman, Sons and Miller, it then reverted to the title of Jackaman & Sons, with H.M. Jackaman in partnership with his son Henry Simon Batley Jackaman until 1925 when H.M. Jackaman's retirement 1eft H.S.B. Jackaman as sole proprietor. Tragically, H.S.B. Jackaman died in 1932, surviving his father by only two years, and the practice was then taken over by Neville Haywood Smith, formerly of Gudgeons Prentice of Stowmarket who continued as sole practitioner and in 1938 changed the name to Jackaman, Sons & Smith It subsequently became Jackaman, Smith & Mulley when Walter Horace Mulley, who had been articled with H.S.B. Jackaman and had worked in London since qualifying as a solicitor in 1932, returned to Ipswich in 1947 and entered into partnership with N. Haywood Smith. In 1951 the

Top: A cheque dated 10th July 1813.
Above: W.H. Mulley, CBE, Partner 1947. Senior Partner 1960-1978.

firm's Felixstowe practice was established in premises at 167/171 Hamilton Road. Silent Street had by this time, been the home of the ipswich offices for well over a century, having undergone significant rebuilding and renovation in 1901; however, in 1958 "Mike" Mulley as he was known, was able to acquire the freehold of Oak House, the magnificent Tudor property at 7 Northgate Street, and the Ipswich branch of the practice has operated from there ever since.

W.H. Mulley retired in 1978 after a distinguished career which included a significant contribution to the water industry, for which he was

awarded a CBE, and an active involvement in local government, serving as a Councillor for the Bixley Ward, as Alderman of the Borough, and as Mayor.

Above: *A picture taken in the first half of the 20th century of Jackaman Smith & Mulley's Tudor offices in Northgate Street, Ipswich.*
Right: *Unveiling the plaque of 'Oak House' in 1977.*

He left the practice in the hands of Walter ("Terry") McBride and Warwick Elwood who had both become partners in 1968, the former having served his articles with W.H. Mulley. Norman Berry and John Pulham also became partners on W.H. Mulley's retirement. In recent years the firm of Jackaman, Smith & Mulley has grown as a result of a number of acquisitions and mergers. First it acquired the practice of J. Noel Cooper & Williamson of Saxmundham in 1976. Then in 1990 it merged with the long established Felixstowe firm of Haward & Ramsey formed some forty years earlier by Lou Cobden-Ramsey and Haywood Haward who were later joined and succeeded by Tony Coles. More recently, in 1997, the specialist residential conveyancing practice of Galey & Wyncoll merged with Jackaman, Smith & Mulley following the death of Galey and the retirement of Wyncoll and the remaining partner in that firm Clive Stamp, became a consultant with Jackaman, Smith & Mulley. Later that same year the Diss firm of Rollin & Co, where P.H. Rollin, who incidentally had also served his articles under W.H. Mulley at Ipswich, was sole practitioner also merged with Jackaman, Smith & Mulley. These mergers brought into the firm Tony Coles who became a partner and retired in 1997 and Peter Rollin who is a current partner. John Fountain became a partner in 1984, Paul McGrath and James Laband in 1991, and Stephen Firmin and Timothy Owers in 1995. In 1998 the Partnership welcomed its first lady partner, James Laband's wife Catherine whose primary task is to advise and assist the older client.

The present partners feel that in the closing decade of the century, people cherish 'old fashioned' values and the service and individual attention that used to be taken for granted. With the impending withdrawal of legal aid in most circumstances and constant change, including the extensive reforms in the Court's approach to litigation as well as increasingly complex legislation from Brussels and Westminster, every effort is made to ensure that clients can obtain specialist legal advice

and assistance close to their homes or places of business. The branches at Ipswich, Felixstowe and Diss therefore provide a gateway affording easy access to the specialist skills of both partners and other qualified staff wherever they may be located.

From its founding, the proprietors of the Firm have been dedicated to the tradition of service to the community. This is demonstrated not only by their involvement in local affairs over the years as coroners, bailiffs, aldermen, mayors, church wardens and other appointees, but also by the esteem and respect of their professional colleagues and the townspeople of Ipswich, as evidenced in the correspondence and documents still in existence. The present partners of Jackaman, Smith & Mulley believe that service to the local community is the principal factor which has enabled the practice to flourish for 200 years. It is recognising this and building on the virtues of their predecessors, as well as embracing the advantages of the technology necessary to thrive in the next millennium the partners hope that the firm will serve the people of Ipswich and Suffolk for at least another 200 years.

Above: *Park House, Mere Street, Diss (the Diss office of Jackaman, Smith & Mulley).*
Below: *The current senior partners of the firm.*

The Galway boy who came in search of a fortune and found one

During the second world war East Anglia played a key role in the Battle of Britain and allied bombing campaigns in Europe. With its Easterly location and gentle landscape the region was the primary choice for new air base construction. Building workers arrived from all parts of the country and settled in the area while working on the airfields. Some of them found that life in East Anglia suited them and decided to remain there after the war. One such man was Mr J T Breheny, who subsequently went on to found the firm of J Breheny Contractors Limited. From modest beginnings, this firm has grown into a well-established, successful concern, carrying out a wide range of prestigious construction projects over a large geographical area and providing secure local employment. Following the company's recent celebration of

its 35th anniversary, this seems an appropriate opportunity to look back over the history of J Breheny Contractors Limited and its founder, Jack Breheny.

Jack Breheny was born in Ireland on 20th November, 1915. His parents had a small farm in Dunmore, County Galway, and Jack, one of seven children, spent his youth working on the family farm. At the age of 21, however, he decided to leave home and seek his fortune in

Right: *John Breheny learning the ropes in 1970.*
Below: *Mr Jack Breheny, left, discussing progress on the A12 Frostenden Bypass, Suffolk in 1964.*

Breheny himself at 251 Long Road, Lowestoft; Betty kept the books and dealt with the administration of the business, including paying the wages. Jack had around a dozen employees and was the proud owner of one digger. Breaking into the market required persistence, as he was in competition with already-established businesses. Most of the early contracts were in the Lowestoft area where Jack was well known, and projects secured during the 60s varied considerably in scope; one of the most significant was the A12 Frosenden bypass, carried out for Suffolk County Council at a cost of £54,000. It was the company's successful involvement in large-scale projects like this one which quickly established its reputation in the industry, a reputation which by the early 1970s was spreading and securing work further afield.

London where he duly arrived in 1936 with only the clothes he was wearing and £2 in his pocket. Despite many construction sites at that time displaying large signs stating 'No Irishmen Need Apply' he found a site which offered him a job at a few pence an hour - making tea. From there Jack progressed from teaboy to labourer, from labourer to bricklayer, and from bricklayer to Contracts Manager on numerous defence projects in the second world war. One of these projects brought him to East Anglia, which has remained his adopted home ever since.

Mr Breheny was employed as Contracts Manager for the civil engineering contractor Ames and then as General Manager for Bowell & Harper's civil engineering division in Lowestoft. It was here that he met Betty, the lady who was later to become his wife.

By the age of 47 Jack Breheny had acquired a great deal of experience within the construction industry and had also built up many good contacts in the Lowestoft area through his involvement at senior level with other civil engineering firms; and in 1963 he decided to start his own business. Of the institutions which he approached for a loan, Barclays Bank in Lowestoft was the only one prepared to lend him £5,000 to support his venture. The company has remained a loyal customer of theirs ever since.

The new firm's original base was the family home built by Mr

In 1973 the company's head office moved from Henstead to a more accessible location on the Lion Barn Industrial Estate at Needham Market, near Ipswich, and before the end of the decade a second office had been opened in Cambridgeshire, where the firm was being increasingly active. The second office was a crucial step in the

operations, coastal defence works and civil airport runway construction. In 1993 Breheny became only the third civil engineering contractor in Britain to successfully achieve accreditation to BS5750. Today, the full range of the company's activities - everything from constructing river and sea defences to installing domestic water meters, from pedestrianising a shopping centre to building an industrial estate, and work on anything from a railway level crossing to a lock on the Broads - are covered by Quality Assurance. The company provides a competitive and reliable service, and a large proportion of its business is repeat orders from customers who are impressed by Breheny's ability to meet specification with high quality workmanship and complete projects on time and to budget.

Jack Breheny died peacefully, with his family by his side, in April 1999 after a long illness. His wife, Betty remains a director of the company and his son, John, is now Chairman. The family firm which he began in 1963 is a fitting testament to a man who worked hard throughout his life and lived life to the full. Current turnover stands in excess of £44million per annum; its workforce consists of some 600 employees, working on sites ranging from Humberside to Kent. With its balance sheet showing over £8million cash reserves and fixed assets which include some 3,000 items of plant, this company represents quite an impressive return from the £2 with which 21 year old Jack set out to find his fortune, all those years ago.

Top left: The West End Road to Princes Street link under construction in 1985. **Below:** *The current head office at Creeting St Mary, near Ipswich.*

company's development strategy. Located in Huntingdon, it was well positioned to work with the Development Corporations at Peterborough and Milton Keynes, where during the 1980s a vast amount of commercial development and new housing was under construction to accommodate the expanding population and offer the inhabitants of London's overcrowded inner city areas, amongst others, the opportunity to make a fresh start. Breheny's at Huntingdon expanded rapidly through its involvement in the development of these newly urbanised areas commissioned by the Development Corporations, as well as local authority schemes.

Meanwhile, at Needham Market the firm's active involvement in highway construction and maintenance continued. Major highways projects during the 1980s included village bypasses at Hadleigh, Ixworth and Saxmundham and a series of trunk road maintenance contracts particularly on the then A45 (A14). In addition, following the award of its first Term Mainlaying Contract for Anglian Water in 1982 the Needham office continued to be responsible for major infrastructure works throughout the decade, and also became involved in Design and Build, undertaking its first £1million design and build project in 1988. Overall, the 1980s were a period of major consolidation and expansion of the company's client base and activities. By 1989 continued expansion led the company to move into a new, purpose built Head Office complex at nearby Creeting St Mary, where on-site facilities included a major vehicle workshop and storage areas for its large plant fleet as well as modern offices. Similar purpose built facilities were provided in Huntingdon the following year.

Success has continued during the 1990s, with the company expanding its range of activities into landfill site

Leading the way in insurance

E nglish insurance companies took off during the heady days of the South Sea Bubble. Although this went down in history as an 18th century speculator's disaster it was the era in which overseas development was protected by insurance cover more sophisticated than that offered by arrangements made over the tables of Lloyd's Coffee House. Insurance companies, like banks and Tontines, were at first small local ventures offering limited scope for investment and protection for specific purposes.

Royal Exchange Assurance was set up in 1720 to provide marine insurance and, soon after, cover for fire and life. Everyone knows the folk tales of early fire insurance schemes when the fire engines belonged to insurance companies who refused to tend the burning houses of non-customers! The great, and risky, days of oriental trade saw a proliferation in every home port of British insurance companies. Many of these

fell by the wayside unable to meet the claims of individual merchants and ship owners ruined by war, tempest, piracy and other local problems.

The Guardian Insurance Company, founded 1821, not only provided insurance cover at home but operated on a Pan-European scale to cater for the needs of the considerable ex-patriate communities of Englishmen and Scots. These not only commanded foreign armies and fleets but established industries and trading houses around the Mediterranean and in the Baltic hinterland of the still primitive Russian Empire. The English clubs, schools and churches set up by these communities took out their insurance with the companies at home which protected their members commercial interests.

These two fore-runners of the Guardian Royal Exchange, like many British marine insurance companies, were hit hard by the 'Alabama' claims following the American Civil War, during which the English built 'commerce raiders' of the innovative CSN had virtually destroyed the American mercantile

Top left: *The Royal Exchange in London pictured in 1900.*
Right: *Suffolk House, (left of picture) the Ipswich headquarters of Guardian Royal Exchange since 1968.*

marine. A prime example of the reasons that cause insurance disclaimers to delete cover for acts of God, war and natural disaster. As time went by both these separate firms absorbed others within their aegis in order to expand their expertise in fields such as burglary and motor car insurance, at one time a very new idea indeed.

Naturally branches were established in the developing colonies to provide cover for South African miners, Australasian sheep stations and tropical planters of all kinds.

British insurance firms during the 20th Century led the way in the invisible 'earnings market' by catering for nations, in South America and elsewhere, which had not yet developed their own commercial infra-structures.

Two World Wars interspersed by a decade of world trade depression bore as heavily on the two insurance companies as on their commercial and private customers, who ultimately pay the bill in higher premiums. Following almost a century of amalgamation with other local and specialist firms the Royal Exchange Group and the Guardian Assurance Group joined in 1968 to become the Guardian Royal Exchange.

It was decided to establish a new headquarters away from London with its staff related problems of costly housing and daily transport. Relocation and 'quality of life' were then the buzz words among companies leaving the choked capital behind. The old seaport of Ipswich, the market and county town of beautiful rural Suffolk was chosen and a clean cut 1950's style building was erected on Civic Drive. The staff who agreed to the move found Ipswich, and its rural and coastal hinterland, provided a pleasant place to dwell. Not only were open air sports easily available but this historic area has a cultural life second to none.

New 3 bedroom homes then cost under £4,000 or around three-quarters of London prices. As some staff were unable to tear themselves away from the delights of London the new HQ has provided continuing employment opportunities for local people. It has since more than doubled the size of its original Civic Drive site and is as much a part of the local scene as older landmarks in the unique architectural styles of East Anglia. Thirty or so years after the move the GRE migrants are so well settled that their children and grand-children are now local folk following family tradition in working for a local company, the Guardian Royal Exchange. The Company was taken over by the French-owned AXA Group in 1999 but the Ipswich headquarters will remain a major location for the group well into the future.

Top left: The Head Office Typing Department pictured in the early 1970s. Top right: Another picture from the early 1970s of the Mortgage Department, on the sixth floor of Suffolk House. Below: The company sports pavilion at Ipswich, formally opened in June 1971 by Mr Bigland, then Managing Director.

Suffolk's supplier of Swedish style

S ay the name H O Cox to anyone in Ipswich today and they will immediately think of cars. But during the first part of the 20th century, the Cox family was known to the locals as a provider not of motors, but of meat. They were butchers, and Hector Orville Cox too became a butcher, working for the family business. His real interest lay in cars and motorbikes, however; he began buying and selling cars during the second world war, and by 1945 he had set up in business at garage premises at 43-45 Wherstead Road, Ipswich.

The garage prospered as car ownership in Ipswich increased, and H O Cox found it necessary to engage more and more mechanics and other staff to work for him; at one stage up to 50 people were employed. By 1950 his business was sufficiently well established for Hector to form a limited company with his brother as co-director. H O Cox was an excellent name, as Hector Orville's brother conveniently shared his initials - Hubert Oswald. The two brothers were joined in the enter- prise by 'Bunny' Bennett, who took care of the two-wheeled side of the business, selling and repairing motorbikes and scooters. How many respectable, settled family men in Ipswich today can still remember buying their first motorbike, or perhaps their first Vespa, from H O Cox, back in the 50s?

Above: St. Peters Street Garage in the 1950s.
Below: Promoting Vespas at Suffolk Show.

Having entered the motor trade through dealing in second-hand cars, the firm then progressed to selling new vehicles, and the first marque which they specialised in was Singer, which in the 1960s became part of the Rootes Group together with other makes such as Humber, Hillman and Sunbeam. Popular family cars of that era included Humber's Hawk and Super Snipe, the Singer Vogue, the Singer Gazelle and the Hillman Minx. The little rear-engined Hillman Imp was quite a novelty, and, in the days before self-service petrol stations, confused many a forecourt attendant upon first acquaintance as there was apparently nowhere to put the petrol (in fact the fuel went in under the "bonnet", which was actually the boot). With its aluminium engine and spritely performance, the boxy little Imp gained many fans; but those customers of Cox's who preferred more streamlined styling would have more likely to buy a Sunbeam Alpine or Rapier. On the light commercial side, Commer held a good share of the market with the Commer Cob and the Commer EDV (Express Delivery Van). There was, however, a gap in the Commer range, which Mr Cox was quick to spot: Commer did not offer a pick-up version. Having identified this gap in the market, Mr Cox seized his opportunity and set about remedying Commer's omission by building his own pick-up body for the Commer van. This venture proved a success; commercial bodybuilding became a lucrative part of the business, and during the early 1960s the firm sold many hundreds of Commer pick-up conversions.

By the end of the decade, however, the Rootes Group was struggling badly and was eventually bought out by Chrysler, at which stage Cox reassessed the situation and, in 1971, transferred to the Saab franchise which it still holds today.

the very highest level of customer satisfaction, and recognises the importance of making sure that all staff are fully skilled in every aspect of their jobs. Such determination towards total professionalism ensures that the company consistently provides an exceptionally high standard of customer care, which led to Cox of Ipswich being named National Winner of the Saab Customer Care Award in 1994. To complement its own excellent record in customer care, the company also knows that the high-class Swedish cars which it sells will meet customers' expectations, as Saab produce some of the best and safest cars in the world.

H O Cox (Car Sales) Ltd will soon celebrate its 50th anniversary. Throughout these years the family firm has consistently met the needs of Suffolk's motorists; for more than half this time it been established as main Saab dealer, and has built up the experience and professionalism necessary not only to compete in today's market place, but to succeed, maintaining an enviable reputation amongst its growing number of customers for getting it right first time, every time.

Top right: *Managing Director, Andrew Cox.*
Below: *The new car showroom in the early 1990s.*

Today the company is based at prestigious, purpose-built premises in Goddard Road East, opened in 1990 and providing comprehensive facilities to meet all customer requirements. The small, highly experienced, family-based team of fourteen is headed by managing director Andrew M Cox, the son of the founder. Andrew Cox is firmly committed to maintaining

Building on the success of previous generations

Even as a little boy, the founder Robert George Carter knew what he wanted to be when he grew up - he wanted to be a carpenter, like his grandfather. And this was the first of many wise decisions which have led to the R G Carter Group becoming the successful, well-respected construction company that it is today.

Young George, as he chose to be called (George was his grandfather's name) became a carpenter's apprentice at the age of 14, practising his new skills with the tools he had inherited from his grandfather. After his apprenticeship he tried life in London, decided it was not for him, and returned to East Anglia, where he spent the next few years working alongside experienced craftsmen who displayed the high level of skill that was to become so important to George.

In 1914 George Carter joined up and served in France. His bravery, which almost cost him his life on a number of occasions, earned him the Military Medal and the Croix de Guerre. Within three days of being demobbed he found employment on a building site in Norwich; he quickly rose to foreman and then to general foreman, and by 1921 he was married and running his own business.

From the outset, the whole family was involved in the venture; his uncles helped him financially, his wife Florence acted as secretary, bookkeeper and wages clerk and her brother Ted drove the horse and trolley, and later the motor lorry. George worked tirelessly to get his business up and running, but always managed to find time for his children, Robert Edward, Betty, Mary and Ruth. Where work was concerned, his guiding rule was that a contract had to be completed on time even if it meant working from six in the morning until ten in the evening during the summer months. When a contract was finished he liked to put up hoardings emblazoned with the firm's proud boast, On Time Again!. He would not tolerate timewasters, but he would reward hard work, and this created great loyalty among his workforce.

Having survived the depression of the late 1920s and early 1930s, George decided in 1932 to turn the firm into a limited company. His son Bob joined R G Carter Limited as an apprentice carpenter six years later, but unfortunately his early career was interrupted, as his

Above: *Coplestone School, Ipswich in 1974.*
Below: *The Lansbury Hotel, Ipswich.*

father's had been, by the outbreak of war. The firm obtained a steady stream of Government contracts; one of the more unusual jobs the construction of a fake city, complete with homes and factories, at Withernsea, as a decoy to draw German bombers away from nearby Hull.

Bob Carter returned in 1946, and took over as managing director in 1950. In the early 50s under Bob Carter's leadership, business began to boom, and by the mid-1950s, R G Carter had become the largest building firm in Norfolk. It was in 1952 that the Carter Group laid foundations for its formal move into Ipswich, with the acquisition of locally respected building firm Blackburns in Harleston. This led to the formation of R G Carter Harleston which in turn expanded into Ipswich, opening an office in Hampton Road in 1972.

The company has been an influence on the Ipswich construction scene since the early 60s, initially building schools for the borough and county local authorities. Among notable landmark projects were the refurbishment of the town's famous

Corn Exchange and the extension of Barclays Bank in Princes Street. The company also constructed Coplestone High School in 1974, and a multi-million pound dispensary and dental clinic for the United States Air Force at the former RAF Bentwaters.

Highlights from the 80s include Woodbridge School and Suffolk County Council's records office. The last decade has seen the construction of many projects within the Ipswich area including the recreation centre at the former RAF Bentwaters (1990); a new hotel for Whitbread on Ransomes Europark and the art block at Suffolk College (both 1991); the Tesco store at Kesgrave and the Euro Retail Park, Ipswich (both 1995); and a major expansion of the Belstead Brook Manor Hotel (1996). In 1998 the company created new hospitality suites for Ipswich Town Football Club.

R G Carter Ipswich expanded into its present site at 50 St Nicholas Street, Ipswich (telephone: 01473 233655) in 1988, whilst maintaining the Hampton Road offices for the small and general works customers.

The Group is currently enjoying the most successful period in its history under the chairmanship of Robert Carter, Bob's son. This family tradition, now in its third generation, is a crucial element in the stability and security of the workforce and the continued expansion and success of the company.

Top left: *The Art and Design Block of Ipswich College.* ***Above:*** *Ransomes Europark, Ipswich.* ***Left:*** *The Recreation Centre, Bentwaters.* ***Below:*** *Belstead Brook Hotel, Ipswich.*

Providing the service and support needed at a time of loss

In 1840 the public was able to benefit from two new services: the Penny Post, and Mr Edward S Singleton's undertaking business. The modern-day equivalents of both are still going strong -today, Funeral Directors, like doctors and vets, are on call at all hours of the day and night to provide a valuable service to those in need at a worrying time.

During the late 19th century lavish funerals were customary amongst the wealthy; in 1892 Ipswich undertakers C Hastings & Son, founded in 1876, charged £6-18s-0d (£6.90) for a polished coffin, breast plate bearers, use of cloaks, closed hearse, two broughams for the family, all cemetery fees and attendance at the funeral.

Less costly options started at £2-10s-0d (£2.50) for an adult funeral and £1-0s-0d for a child's. As a comparison, the cost of a bespoke gentleman's suit at that time would have been around £3. It used to be said that a funeral, a wedding and a holiday all cost about the same, but the relative cost of funerals has decreased; a late-20th century funeral costs on average between £1,200 and £1,500, whereas we spend anywhere between £7,000 and £10,000 on a wedding.

junction of Woodbridge Road and Samuel Road. The two Ipswich firms were merged into Singleton & Hastings located at Berners Street, while their Felixstowe branch continued to trade as Farthings. During the following decade the nature of the funeral business began to change as many small independent firms were bought by large national companies, which were in turn acquired by multi-national companies in the 1990s. Determined to remain both independent and competitive, the Farthing family decided to embark on an investment programme to refurbish their offices at Felixstowe and move the Ipswich side into purpose-built premises. Locating a suitable site proved difficult, but eventually a plot of land on Woodbridge Road met their requirements, and the firm opened brand new offices at Deben House in late 1993 trading under the altered name of Farthing, Singleton and Hastings. The building was carefully designed to provide separate access for bereaved families and a tranquil and relaxed environment for visiting. There are private Chapels of Rest, a small service Chapel which will seat up to 20, and a display room where customers can choose from a selection of coffins. Other

The Farthing family's involvement in undertaking began in 1954 in the Felixstowe area, when Stanley Farthing, by trade a builder, expanded into the undertaking business. His son Donald took this part of the business over, and was joined in 1960 by his wife Margaret. Donald and Margaret came to Ipswich in 1960 when they acquired Hastings & Son. In 1975 they took over the firm of Singleton's, which had been handed down through at least four generations of the Singleton family and was sited at the

Top: *An invoice dated 1892.*
Right: *The funeral of a Policeman in the 1920s.*

all its staff are fully qualified, and as befits such a highly professional firm it maintains an active involvement in various trade organisations. Donald Farthing is a former National President of the National Association of Funeral Directors, and Luke continues this interest, serving on the Board of Examiners as well as representing the local area. Membership of the Society of Allied & Independent Funeral Directors helps the firm face the growing threats from the large organisations; and Farthing, Singleton & Hastings was recently honoured to be invited to join the elite organisation of National Selected Morticians, which boasts less than 50 members throughout Europe. Membership is by invitation only and the demonstrated ability to maintain excellent standards of service is a pre-requisite.

services include floristry, a comprehensive monumental masonry service provided through sister company F Masters of Woodbridge, custom-printed mourning stationery such as Order of Service cards, acknowl-edgement cards and announcement cards, and a chauffeur-driven fleet of E-class Mercedes vehicles.

Farthing, Singleton & Hastings, first as separate firms and then as a unified business, share a common history of providing an excellent level of service through dedicated and compassionate staff. This tradition continues today, with the emphasis placed on continuous personal contact with the funeral director who takes responsibility for a family's instructions. Exceptionally, the firm has lady funeral directors, a move made in response to society's changing expectations. Farthing, Singleton & Hastings have been at the forefront of various innovative practices designed to meet the clients' increasing demands for individually-tailored funeral services, having also estab-lished its own pre-payment funeral plan (Golden Security) and its own in-house masonry service. Other requests, such as the provision of special willow (woven) coffins for 'Green' funerals, can also be met.

The firm is committed to providing the highest level of service and support to bereaved clients;

As a family firm, Farthing, Singleton & Hastings' future is in the local community, where it will continue to offer the best possible service to the families of East Suffolk, expertly and sympathetically tailored to any budget The Ipswich branch of Farthing, Singleton & Hastings is today principally run by Luke Farthing, who became part of the family firm in 1985, and the Felixstowe branch by his brother Robert who has been with the firm since 1973, while parents Donald and Margaret remain partners in the business.

Above: Luke Farthing conducting a horse-drawn funeral at Grundisburgh near Ipswich.
Below left: The 'Topping out' ceremony of Deben House, 1993. Below: Luke, Margaret, Donald and Robert Farthing under the Singleton Tree in Ipswich Cemetery.

The innovative company that doesn't let grass grow under its feet

Next time you get your lawnmower out - or listen to your neighbours using theirs - you may like to consider that the original technological concept of the mechanical lawnmower was derived from cloth shearing equipment, and that the first mowing machine was manufactured in Ipswich in 1832.

The company responsible was Ransomes, and its founder was Robert Ransome, a Quaker from Norwich who, by using his natural ingenuity and the knowledge he had gained during his apprenticeship, had made a name for himself by designing and manufacturing agricultural machinery, particularly ploughs. He had patented an iron roofing tile in 1783, followed some 18 months later by a patent for tempered cast iron plough shares, an invention of great value to farmers. In 1789 he came to Ipswich, invested £200 in setting up a foundry in an old malting, and in March of that year placed an advertisement in the Ipswich Journal advising local farmers that they could obtain Ransome's patent cast iron plough shares, also plough wheels, harrow teeth, coulters, gate irons etc, 'for READY MONEY' from his new iron and brass foundry opposite St Mary at the Key Church.

The ingenuity and innovation which were features of the company's products from the very beginning continued; at first his chief interest lay in developing better and better machinery for the agricultural community, who greeted each new idea with enthusiasm. Then in 1818 Stoke Bridge was swept away by floods, and the individual sections for the new iron bridge were cast at Ransomes' foundry; this bridge remained in good condition for over 100 year. At around the same time Ransomes became involved in Ipswich's gas lighting scheme.

The founder had been joined by sons James and Robert, and by the time of his retirement in 1825 the firm was employing around 60 men and boys. A charming example of the friendly atmosphere of the firm is the tradition of masters and men

sitting around the embers of the last furnace on New Year's Eve, sharing bread, cheese and beer, swapping tales, singing songs and exchanging jokes.

It was in 1832 that Ransomes acquired the licence to manufacture the very first mechanical lawn mower, and thereafter began making them at a rate of some 70 to 80 mowers a year. This was also the era of the steam engine and the railway; the company played an important role in the development of the latter between 1836 and 1869, manufacturing chilled iron crossings, switches and other components and assisting with bridge and station construction. Meanwhile, the company's first portable steam engine for agricultural use was exhibited in 1841, and from there Ransomes went on to develop a range of self-moving and stationary engines, used initially for threshing, milling and chaff-cutting and later for industrial use as well. Steam-powered machinery, particularly the threshing machine, was to remain central to the firm's activities until the late 1930s, when the internal combustion engine rendered steam power obsolete, and from 1945 Ransomes was perhaps best known for its combine harvesters.

Meanwhile, the manufacture of grass mowers had continued, with their design undergoing continual improvement; the petrol engine was added in 1902, and in 1926 the company launched the first electrically-powered

*Top left: The founder Robert Ransome. **Top right:** A page from a sales leaflet in 1883. **Left:** Ransomes Patent 'Gear Automaton' at work in 1897.*

RANSOMES' Lawn Mowers
THE BEST in the WORLD

THE "AUTOMATONS" AND "ANGLO-PARIS"

mower. Other early 20th century diversifications included the manufacture of the FE 2B biplane aircraft during the first world war, and the launch of Britain's first battery-powered electric truck in 1920; and in 1964 Ransomes introduced the world's first tractor-mounted power-driven 5 unit gang mower.

In 1987 the company took the decision to concentrate exclusively on grass equipment, an area in which it is now an acknowledged world leader. In recent years Ransomes' tradition of innovation has continued, consolidating its expertise and continuing to grow through product development; since 1994 the company has introduced more new products in a shorter time frame than any of its competitors, and can truly claim to have the most up-to-date, innovative and complete range on the market.

On 27th January 1998 Ransomes was acquired by Textron Inc, one of America's largest and best-performing multi-

industries, with interests in the golf and turf-care industry. As part of Textron, Ransomes is now securely placed to ensure economic value in a competitive world. True to its pedigree of pioneering engineering excellence, Ransomes is still leading the way with innovations such as the first all-electric greens mower for the golf industry, and the first fairway machines to use biodegradable fluids. The history of this Suffolk company lay in making machinery designed to work the land more effectively; its future as a major international manufacturer lies in delivering products which offer productivity, perfection, operator comfort and safety, and environmental care.

Top: A delightful dealer sign advertising Ransomes mowers at the end of the 19th Century.
Left: Assembling 'Ajax' hand mowers in 1966.
Below: One of the early Ransomes Hydraulic 5/7 gang mowers, the first of its type in the world, 1967.

The Society that taught habits of economy and saving

Over the last 150 years the Building Society movement has had a tremendous impact on the pattern of the nation's domestic financial arrangements. Today, many a child is introduced to the basics of financial planning at an early age by having a building society account opened in its name by parents or grandparents. In 1849 Mr Richard Dykes Alexander, the first President of the new Ipswich and Suffolk Freehold Land Society, broke new ground when he expressed the hope that the new movement 'would teach (the working classes) habits of economy and saving' - the Society would also give them the opportunity to become the owner of a freehold plot of land which also conferred the right to vote.

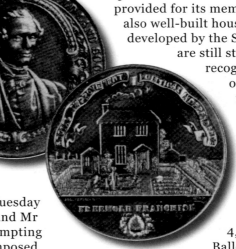

had been taken up, making Ipswich the fastest-growing of all the various Societies which were being started up around the country, with the exception of Derby. At the end of the first year receipts amounted to £4,936.13s.0d; 98.5 acres of land had been purchased at Cauldwell Hall Estate, divided into 282 allotments and offered to senior members at £21 10s 0d each, and the Society had begun to fulfil its purpose.

There were problems. This initial site was at the time an outlying area of fields and pasture, and was thought to be much too far away from Ipswich. The original system of offering available plots to the longest serving members discouraged new investors, and was replaced by a ballot system in 1958. The Society continued to grow steadily, and in its first 50 years of existence the Society took £809,000 and acquired and allotted 133 estates. From 1866 it provided for its members not only land, but also well-built houses. Many of the areas developed by the Society in those early days are still standing today and are recognisable by the intials FLS on the stone nameplate at first floor level. During the next 70 years, the artisan classes were enjoying healthier and better housing conditions, and the Corporation was being pressured into buying better services. In 1899 4,692 members went into Ballot for 53 properties or plots of land. Houses in Philip Road, Ipswich were available for the sum of £275. If a Mortgage was needed that was also provided. The

During the mid-1800s Ipswich, with its new Wet Dock, its expanding rail network, its malting, brewing, silk-weaving and brickmaking industries, its market and its garrison, was a fast-growing town in terms of both population and prosperity. The Alexander family was one of the important local families, having in 1840 given to the town a Temperance Hall - the building in which the first public meeting of the new Society took place, on Tuesday 4th December 1849. The Hall was packed, and Mr Alexander explained the imaginative and tempting principles of the Society to an audience composed mainly of working men: for a modest subscription of as little as 1s 6d a week, the working man could within five or six years become the owner of a plot of land, which at the time brought the right to vote.

At that first meeting 140 members were enrolled and 150 shares taken. Thirteen weeks later 732 shares

Top: *A map dated 1899 of Freehold land developed by the Society.* ***Above:*** *The medal struck in memory of founder James Taylor.*

May we help you to buy your house

The money waits

Full particulars of the
FREEHOLD LAND SOCIETY
The Ipswich and Suffolk Permanent Benefit Building Society
44 UPPER BROOK STREET
IPSWICH

Society's influence spread far beyond Ipswich with large developments in many towns including Felixstowe and Lowestoft.

It was during the 1930s that housing development took off in an unprecedented manner, with the devel-

opment of whole new estates such as Martlesham and Kesgrave. The second world war brought a halt to building work and damage to existing homes, and the Society advanced funds to repair damaged homes when peace returned.

During the 70s and 80s home ownership was firmly established as the social ideal and building societies played an increasingly central part in the national economy. As their role evolved, the tendency was for small societies to combine, through mergers and takeovers, until the original 2,000 societies became 70 larger ones. Ipswich Building Society, with its reputation for service, efficiency and reliability and its roots in the Suffolk community, resulted from the merger of the Ipswich and District and the Ipswich and Suffolk in 1975, and since that time it has opened more branches and continually updated its range of accounts to maintain its competitive edge. Currently it has assets of about a quarter of a billion pounds, and 21 offices serving over 40,000 members. As it reaches its 150th anniversary the Ipswich Building Society, served by the latest computer technology, staffed by uniformed staff and handling thousands of transactions a month, may seem to have changed a great deal - yet, as it continues to offer its members imaginative and tempting ways to become homeowners or to invest their money, it is, in a sense, still fulfilling the same vital function as the 'Old Freehold' did, so many years ago.

Left: *A poster advertising the Society in the 1950s.*
Below: *Part of the General Office pictured in the late 1940s.*

The furniture craftsmen of Back Hamlet

Laurence Titchmarsh and Gordon Goodwin, brothers-in-law, set up as furniture manufacturers in May 1920. Laurence was the accountant and Gordon was an ex-soldier turned furniture designer which proved a useful combination when the partners took over Lomax and Childs. This old firm of joiners and cabinet makers operated, appropriately enough, from Roundwood, formerly home of Admiral Lord Nelson who had defended Britain in wooden warships.

The new partnership aimed at the better end of the market for which Gordon Goodwin designed some of the most popular high quality reproduction furniture made between the wars. Their early accounts show the true value of the pound in the 1920s when wages for their first week totalled £14 including 1/- overtime paid to T Sharp. Hand operated two man pit saws were then still in use at a time when the first year's trading was worth £1,349 giving a loss of over £161.

After five years the firm moved to a builder's yard in Back Hamlet which cost £665, then equivalent to a generous annual salary for a banker or a land agent. They were joined by a new Works Manager, Mr S Twiddy, who was a recruit from E Gomme of High Wycombe. Gordon Goodwin, the designer, enjoyed 60% of the profit of around £1,000 from total sales worth £14,623 in 1925. Skilled craftsmen or journeymen received 1s 3d (6p) an hour and worked, on average, 65 hours a week to earn £3-18s-9d (£3.90) a week, £200 a year was a very good wage in the mid-twenties. Everyone worked on Saturday mornings - and Woolworths sold nothing over sixpence in price.

In common with other employers of the era Titchmarsh and Goodwin organised annual works outings to seaside resorts, which, in the days before paid holidays became normal, were extremely popular. The low sales of the famous London furniture shop, Waring and Gillow, caused some concern amongst suppliers like Titchmarsh and Goodwin. In 1929 Gordon Goodwin wed Winifred Edwards and built a handsome home used both in the company catalogue and in advertising Wolseley cars to the well heeled. The next year Titchmarsh and Goodwin bought the first of many fire extinguishers. Trading figures in 1930 rose to £23,213 when the showrooms in Glasgow cost £5 a year in rent!

Gordon Goodwin took over the firm single handed when the partners separated in 1931 the year before his first son Jeremy James was born. Three years later Titchmarsh and Goodwin made panelling and furniture, including a handsome 26 foot (approx. 8M) long oak Refectory or Hall table, for Worksop College. The success of

Top: *Roundwood, once home to Lord Nelson. Titchmarsh and Goodwin's workshops were situated behind the house.* ***Left:*** *The firm's premises pictured in 1925, the office and workshop can be seen on the top left.*

and petrol was severely rationed.

In 1939 Gordon married Gweneth Alderton and rented showrooms in London for an annual rental of £300. These were lavishly appointed to show beautiful period oak furniture and panelling in appropriate baronial surroundings only months before the outbreak of war. The majority of the workforce were conscripted into the armed forces while the few that were left were directed to rival cabinet makers F Tibbenhams! Only two years later the London showrooms were totally destroyed in the 'Blitz'.

the company in making top quality reproduction furniture was not reflected when Titchmarsh and Goodwin tried their hand at the Modernistic style in 1935 to produce plain simple items, in good woods, similar to wartime 'Utility' and 1950s Festival of Britain models. The Titchmarsh and Goodwin clients were not ready for such stark designs. Winifred Goodwin gave birth to Guy Stephen, their second son in this year at a time when Gordon was employing a staff of 138, including 22 wood carvers.

As the famous, strictly rationed 'Utility' furniture was made, elsewhere, for newly weds and families that had been bombed out Titchmarsh & Goodwin were unable to obtain sufficient supplies to keep going. The business was shut down until after the war when continued rationing of timber, and everything else, made furniture making so difficult that the company diversified into buying, at give-away prices, and

Titchmarsh and Goodwin craftsmen travelled all over the country to install staircases, flooring and panelling for the wealthy customers seeking to provide a totally designed setting for the beautiful dressers, tables and desks which they bought from Titchmarsh and Goodwin agents. Other clients making large purchases were hotels and breweries buying for hotels. A third son, Roger Gordon, was born to the Goodwins, in 1936 the year that the family Rover was replaced by an Essex Terraplane at a cost of £117-10s-0d - then a year's wages for many. The later thirties saw Winifred Goodwin die. The company bought its first motor lorry, at a second-hand cost of £10, for deliveries. The same Ford was, in 1943, sold for £20 at a time when vehicles were hard to get

Top left: A works outing to Yarmouth in 1928.
Below: A corner of the sumptuous showrooms in London which opened in 1939.

repairing antiques for resale to people desperate to obtain good quality furniture. Journeymen's wages rose from 1/-11d (10p) per hour in 1941 to 2/-9d (14p) an hour in 1949 when letter post was soon to rise to 2d.(1p).

This brightly confident decade was marked by the first post-war London Furniture Exhibition, a free market for un-rationed goods and the first post war export of Titchmarsh and Goodwin furniture to the USA. The company introduced its Green Label, 'Utility' grade furniture which was finished by being sprayed, rather than hand polished, to reduce costs. The firm made its own half timbered pick-up body for an Austin A40 and installed a dust extraction plant in the workshops. Customers included Emperor Haile Selassie of Ethiopia, the Saudi royal family and King Haakon of Norway, another wartime ally, and the Government of British Honduras buying a desk for HRH Princess Margaret.

The Swinging Sixties saw the purchase of the company's first electric typewriter and the subsequent replacement of the faithful Kalamazoo Payroll System by a Burroughs Sensimatic Account Machine, later replaced by computers. In the works traditional tools in the hands of craftsmen were

assisted by power tools while methods remained little changed. A daring robbery by thieves who used the company van for their get-away was balanced by a contract to re-gild chairs from Buckingham Palace, one of which was damaged in a fire at the works.

Throughout the changes wrought by time Titchmarsh and Goodwin have continued to maintain traditional standards of time consuming craftsmanship for private and corporate clients willing to wait for the best furniture made.

Top left: *A Ford Thames pantechnicon PV.9978 purchased in 1950. The late Ken Dean is in the drivers seat and in the truck are the Goodwin brothers - Roger, Guy, Jeremy and Peter with a friend.*
Top right: *The Mayor of Ipswich, Mike Mulley is shaking the hand of father Goodwin who is flanked by his two sons, Jeremy the eldest to his right and Peter to his left.* ***Below:*** *The staff gathered together to celebrate 75 years of Titchmarsh and Goodwin.*

The business legacy of a well-known 19th century Suffolk family

A hundred and ten years in business have taken the firm, quite literally, from the quill to the computer, and it is this enthusiasm for progress, adopting the latest technology and adapting to changing times and requirements, which has kept Ensors ahead. Today, clients encompass not

In 1889, when taxes were 6d (two and a half new pence) in the £, Isaac Lott Ensor qualified as a Chartered Accountant and became one of the earliest members of the newly-established Institute of Chartered Accountants. Isaac was a member of a well-known Suffolk family; his father, John Lott Ensor, had served the local community as a Liberal Councillor and held various positions of eminence, including appointments as Director of the Ipswich Permanent Benefit Building Society and Guardian of the Ipswich Union. As befitted a business which bore such a highly-respected family name, the accountancy firm of Ensors was founded on the sound basis of personal and prompt service to clients - a never-forgotten policy under which the firm has grown and prospered ever since.

Isaac was joined in due course by his son Lionel, and the name of the firm was changed to I L Ensor & Son; a second branch was opened under the name of Ensor Son & Goult in Bury St Edmunds in 1923 and run by partner Garfield Goult. The Ipswich office moved from Museum Street to Elm Street in 1956; from there it moved to Saxon House in St Nicholas Street in 1980, and in 1988 further expansion led it down the street to Cardinal House, its current home. Cardinal House stands on the former site of the Ipswich Hippodrome Theatre, built in 1905 by Edward Bostock and designed by Frank Matcham (who also designed the London Palladium).

Now known simply as Ensors, the firm has 13 partners and over 120 staff at its six offices throughout Suffolk.

only private individuals but the whole spectrum of businesses in East Anglia: commerce, the professions, transport and shipping, agriculture, charities and pension schemes.

The firm's aim is to remain a flexible, progressive and friendly business which will continue to serve the needs of the East Anglian people and their businesses. The present senior partner is Michael Goldsmith. A committed Ipswich Town FC supporter, a keen bowls player and a former pupil of Northgate Grammar School, Michael has been with the practice since 1970. Prior to joining Ensors he worked for the Inland Revenue - regrettably, collecting tax at a rate somewhat higher than 6d in the £!

***Top left:** The Ipswich Hippodrome Theatre in St Nicholas Street shortly after it opened in 1905.*
***Top right:** Cardinal House, Ensors Ipswich office on the site of the old Hippodrome Theatre.*
***Right:** Michael Goldsmith, Senior Partner of the firm.*

The Ipswich inter-schools events of June 1965 at Broom Hill

Acknowledgments

Ipswich Evening Star

Ipswich Town FC

David Kindred

Thanks are also due to
Peggy Burns for penning the editorial text
and Margaret Wakefield and Mike Kirke for their copywriting skills